J. H Bloomfield

A Cuban Expedition

J. H Bloomfield

A Cuban Expedition

ISBN/EAN: 9783337323622

Printed in Europe, USA, Canada, Australia, Japan

Cover: Foto ©Andreas Hilbeck / pixelio.de

More available books at **www.hansebooks.com**

London:
DOWNEY AND CO.,
YORK STREET, COVENT GARDEN, W.C.
1896.
[*All rights reserved.*]

PREFACE.

THE reader who looks for an exact description of Cuba, its scenery and productions, in the following pages will be disappointed. The Author passed the few months he spent there as a soldier in one of the unfortunate expeditions that have landed on its shores.

The West Indies have been the scene of many daring adventures and cruel sufferings in times past, and the island of Cuba has been pre-eminent in that respect. What lives have been wasted and sufferings endured, in abortive attempts of the people to separate themselves from Spain, will probably never be known.

The Author, when a boy, took part, as narrated in the text, in one of the expeditions whose object was to assist the Cubans in their struggle for independence; like many youths, he was eager for adventure, and when the proposal was made to him, shortly after his arrival in America, he accepted it.

He does not pretend to know much about the political differences between the Cubans and the Mother Country; he simply relates his experience as a soldier and a sailor, in its naked reality, and stripped of the glamour of romance which some people like to throw round everything relating to a life of adventure.

CONTENTS.

CHAPTER I.

The *Darthula* — The expedition sails — At sea — Our Colonel makes a speech—Recruits sea-sick—A man overboard—Running before a gale 1

CHAPTER II.

Barney—His story—Blackbird catching—The "Isle of Pines"—The slaver's hidden money—Yarns . . 12

CHAPTER III.

Arrival on the coast of Cuba—Chased by a war steamer—Short of coal—Run for the Mosquito coast—Wood-cutting — March inland — An Indian village and women—Polygamy and Polyandry 23

CHAPTER IV.

Barney—His story—Tempted to desert—Barney's plan—His idea of happiness 36

CHAPTER V.

My first smoke — Barney's plan frustrated — We sail again—Blewfields—Sick—Attempt to land at Cuba —Chased by a war brig—Under fire—Threatened mutiny—Boat shot away 50

CHAPTER VI.

We outmanœuvre the brig—Run in at night—Disembark men and arms—March for the interior—First encounter with the enemy—Sick men—Quartered at a sugar-mill—Pursuit of lighters on the river— Coopering—We decide to make a raft . . . 67

CHAPTER VII.

The *Ingenio*—A lesson in fortification—We intend to march on Bayamo—Comandante Fernandez—The Chigoe—Men dying—Party of enemy appear—We are sent in pursuit—Sufferings in a swamp—We find the enemy and lose two officers—Rumoured defeat of Cubans in the mountains 82

CHAPTER VIII.

Burial of our officers—Our first prisoners—Return to the *Ingenio*—Arrive in time to take part in the fight 97

CHAPTER IX.

Changes—Ridley sick—Messengers from the junta request us to hurry forward—We evacuate the mill— On the march—Mule-driving—Storey's plan—Dead men—Captains Ryan and Wingate 104

CONTENTS.

CHAPTER X.

Marching through forest—Shooting a Spanish scout—Attack on our rear—Enemy following us—Our chiefs decide to wait for them—Ride ahead and select our ground—Prepare for battle . . . 113

CHAPTER XI.

Thunder, lightning, and rain—Sitting in a wet ditch—The enemy — A trying situation — Battle in the forest — Enemy beaten — Two guns captured — Prisoners shot 123

CHAPTER XII.

Death of Ridley—Pursuit of enemy—Capture of waggons—March on San Jacinto—Assault and capture of San Jacinto—I am wounded—Capture of horses and mules—Promoted 135

CHAPTER XIII.

San Jacinto—Spanish roofs—Fernandez leaves us with one of the guns—Ditching—Shower-baths—Spanish troops—Besieged — Dig out old guns — Mounting gun on church tower—Enemy reconnoitring—We drive them back—We open fire—Gun bursts . . 141

CHAPTER XIV.

The enemy attack—They fall back—They attack again—Repulse of the enemy—Out at night looking for food — Astray—Spanish sentries — Going to die—Thoughts of home—I get my bananas—Get back safely 158

CHAPTER XV.

Enemy reinforced with artillery—They open fire—Shells bursting in the *plaza*—Death of Hodson—The night march—Overtaken by the enemy—Defeated—Escape wounded — My horse saves me — Captain Ryan wounded—Death of Storey. 176

CHAPTER XVI.

A friendly planter—Curing the sick—Shift our quarters —Rest—I get well—Men get lock-jaw—On the march again—A thunderstorm—The "Isla"—Safety 195

CHAPTER XVII.

Shooting deer and pigeons—A pigeon-roost—Ball practice on alligators— Surprised by the enemy — A cavalry charge—Thrown from my horse and roll into the river—A swim for life—Our leader and half our number missing—Escape through a swamp . 209

CHAPTER XVIII.

Resting in the forest—Using fruit for ointment—Presence of mind, which treats of Spanish America . 223

CHAPTER XIX.

We reach the coast—Cocoa-nuts and their owner—Shipwrecked sailors—Trinidad and Casilda—We stop in time—In rags—Hiding in the mangrove swamp— Ships in harbour—We swim off to one—Reception on board 231

CHAPTER XX.

The captain agrees to take two—He promises to place the others—Ashton and I are transferred to the *Tyrer*—The Scotch skipper — Our wretched condition—Quartered with the apprentices . . . 244

CHAPTER XXI.

Loading mahogany—Dreams—Christmas — Decorating the ship—A drunken crew—The soup tureen—The skipper comes aboard—His homily to the steward . 250

CHAPTER XXII.

Sailors' songs—The forecastle poet—Our comrades shout farewell — Go on shore — Trinidad — Speak with Spanish soldiers—The war over—Drunken Englishmen—Cuba, good night 265

CHAPTER XXIII.

Getting under weigh — Homeward-bound — Sailors' shanties—At sea—The Isle of Pines—Cape San Antonio 279

CHAPTER XXIV.

Going north—Cold weather—Hardships of a sailor's life—Reefing topsails—Calling the watch—In the Channel—Painting ship—Towing up the Thames—In dock—Ashton starts for home—My relations . 286

A CUBAN EXPEDITION.

CHAPTER I.

The *Darthula*—The expedition sails—At sea—Our Colonel makes a speech—Recruits sea-sick—A man overboard—Running before a gale.

IN the interval from the death of Narciso Lopez in 1851, to the insurrection headed by Cespedes, Alvarez, Garcia, and others in 1868, Cuba was supposed to be at peace. There is no account of any rising during these seventeen years, yet there were two if not more in that time; in fact, I doubt if the island was ever thoroughly pacified.

Seven years after the shooting of Colonel Crittenden and his companions, in Havana, another expedition was equipped with men and arms from the United States; the barque *Darthula* was loaded with arms and ammunition in an American port, and 285 men, of whom the writer was one, embarked in the same vessel while she lay in New York harbour.

It was late in the evening when I went on board the vessel, and found myself amongst a crowd of young fellows of from eighteen to twenty-five years of age, who had engaged themselves to join the ranks of the patriot army in Cuba.

In all that crowd I did not know a single one. I walked here and there among them, looking and listening for some sign by which I could claim an acquaintanceship with some of them, but they were all strangers to me. I recognised some as countrymen by their accent, but they were not such as I should choose as intimates, and I began to realise that I had associated myself with some very doubtful characters. When I grew tired of watching them, and looking about the decks, I went below to the ship's 'tween decks, and found them fitted up with rough bunks, roughly put together, of sawn pine lumber, and having nothing to do I threw myself into one of them, and placing my little parcel of clothing, all I was possessed of, under my head for a pillow, I was soon fast asleep.

I was awakened early next morning before daylight, by hearing some one at my feet getting sick, and I knew at once, from the motion of the ship, that we were under weigh. I must have slept soundly, notwithstanding my hard bed, for I never heard the noise usually made on board ship in getting the anchor up, or in making sail.

I turned out as I had turned in, all standing, as a sailor would say, and went on deck. The day was beginning to dawn, and there were already little groups of men scattered about the decks; they had been on deck all night, and most of them had not been below since they came on board. They stood there talking and looking over the vessel's side, and watching the land now sinking out of sight; the greater number of them were looking on it for the last time, for of all the men who landed in Cuba on that expedition, only seven, to my knowledge, left it. A good many of them had left comfortable homes, or had given up a useful calling or profession, and bright prospects, to become volunteer soldiers and see the world.

The ship we were embarked in was a clipper-built barque-rigged vessel, with auxiliary steam power, that was only to be used in cases of necessity; there was no funnel to be seen on her deck or anything to indicate that she was a steam vessel, for the opening was covered over, and the funnel itself was stowed away below, but it could be got up and placed in position when necessary at any time.

Before sunrise the crew began to wash the decks, and we were invited to assist, and willingly did so, and soon had everything clean and tidy on deck.

Some more of our men now began to make their appearance from below, looking very sick and woebegone after their first night at sea, and when all of them had come up we were mustered and divided into messes of ten men each by the officers of the ship. We had not yet seen our own officers; probably they were like some of the men, sea-sick on their first night out. There were a few Cubans on the quarter-deck in the early part of the morning, for like most natives of tropical countries, they were early risers, but they disappeared below as soon as we began to wash the decks.

With the wind on the quarter, a fair wind, orders were given to rig out stunsail booms and get stunsails ready for setting, and some of our men, to show their willingness to assist in everything, ran up the rigging with the crew, and helped them to rig out the booms and set the sails; and before eight bells, the breakfast hour, the ship was under every stitch of canvas it was possible to crowd on her; but this did not last long, for at midday the wind having drawn abeam and freshened, the yards had to be braced up a little, and the lower stunsails taken in. An hour later in came topgallant and topmast stunsails, and another pull had to be taken on the lee braces, but all the staysails were now set; this was evidently the ship's best sailing trim, for she seemed to fly through the water, every sail full and rounded, every thread and ropeyarn pulling its utmost, and dragging the beautifully modelled hull through the comparatively smooth water at a twelve-knot pace.

After dinner, or the midday meal, we were all called on deck, where we found our officers already assembled. One of them, a tall, soldierly-looking man, Colonel Ridley, our commander, addressed us, and described the nature and climate of the country to which we were going, the object of the expedition, the difficulties we would have to contend against, the character of the enemy we had to meet, and impressed on us the urgent necessity of strict discipline, and obedience to our officers, for without it, he said, we should only be a rabble, a danger and an encumbrance to our friends, and despicable in the eyes of our enemies. We were, he said, part of a larger force, the vanguard; the main body would soon follow, and be well supplied with munitions and all necessaries for carrying on a successful campaign; there was neither time nor opportunity for giving us the drill and instruction necessary to enable us to meet on equal terms the regular troops of Spain, but he had great faith in our pluck and enthusiasm in a good cause. He had, he said, led men as young and as raw as we were in the Mexican War, and led them to victory, and he hoped to do the same with us; he told us that there was a large creole army already in the field, that we would be received with open arms by the people we were going to fight for, and should our efforts be successful, as he hoped they would be, what a brilliant future was before us!—the certainty of obtaining substantial rewards, and good positions in the army and navy of the new republic.

We were divided into three watches, one of which was always to be on deck to assist the crew in working the ship, and to be exercised and instructed in the use of their arms.

As the afternoon wore on, the wind increased steadily, and sail after sail had to be taken in, and as the wind drew ahead at the same time that it increased in violence, the yards were braced sharp up, until at sundown the ship was close-hauled, under double-reefed topsails, and plunging into a nasty head sea. I happened to be on the lee side of the deck when she made one of her plunges, taking in a great deal of water over her bows, and along the lee side, and I was surprised to feel it warm as it ran over my feet; its temperature must have been several degrees higher than the air, and was probably caused by the Florida Gulf Stream, although not twenty hours from New York. I had read of the Gulf Stream running along the coast of Florida for a short distance, and when it cleared the Bahama reefs and shoals, trending away to the eastward, and of a cold Arctic current running along the east coast of North America; but if that was the case, the cold current must be very narrow, and run close in-shore, and the warm Florida current must run much further north than was thought, or how account for the warm water we were sailing through?

A good many of the men who had joined the expedition were young sailors who were out of employment, and joined simply as they would join, or ship, in a vessel for a cruise or the voyage; they were, of course, quite at home on board ship, and they subsequently proved the best men in the expedition, but there were a great many on board who were now at sea for the first time in their lives, and they were miserably sea-sick. Thus passed our first day at sea. Twice during the night the hands were turned out to shorten sail, as the wind increased, and at sunrise it was blowing a howling gale; the ship was hove to, under a close-reefed main-topsail and fore-topmast staysail, and a heavy head sea was running.

This was the kind of weather to take some of the enthusiasm out of our recruits; those among them who were not helplessly sea-sick, were squeamish and listless, unable to move about and indifferent as to what became of them; some were wishing that they had never left home, while the sailors endeavoured to comfort them by telling them that they would forget it all as soon as we got into fine weather, and not a few, the hardened ones, laughed at their misery.

The gale continued all day and the following

night, but by daylight it had moderated a little and hauled aft, so that it was a fair wind for us once more, and at sunrise the ship was got before it, with the foresail reefed and set, and away we went once more like a racehorse, tearing through the water on our course.

To-day, we had our first misfortune. It was between half-past eleven and twelve in the forenoon, one watch was already at dinner, when an order was given to shake a reef out of the fore-topsail; there was a heavy sea running, and the captain of the vessel was afraid it might break over our quarter, and wished to get more way on the ship to keep her ahead of the seas, and avoid being pooped. Two men jumped aloft to obey the order, and had already let go the reef-points and earings, and were on their way down, when one of them—it is supposed, for no one was looking at him at the time—slipped, or missed his footing on the foot-rope, or Flemish hawse, in coming in, and fell from the yard-arm into the sea.

The man at the wheel shouted, "A man overboard," and lifting a life-buoy that hung near the binnacle, he threw it into the sea after him; every one on deck ran to the side to see him come up astern, and some of us ran up the rigging to watch him. The poor fellow struck out, for he could swim well, but in a few minutes he was out of sight astern, although his voice still reached us, calling on us not to forsake him; but there was such a sea running at the time that it would endanger the ship and all on board to attempt to bring her to the wind, so the poor fellow was left to his fate.

I cannot explain my feelings at the time, when I saw no attempt made to save him. I felt dazed; surely, I thought, they are not going to leave him to drown without making some effort to save him?

I had gone up the main rigging, when the alarm was given, with some of the men, and was just under the top, and holding on to the futtock shrouds, and looking astern at the poor struggling lad, as he appeared on the crest of every sea; an old sailor, one of the crew, was beside me, when I turned to him and asked, "Why don't the captain give some order —can nothing be done to save that man? Is there no possibility of saving him?"

The sailor shook his head.

"Have you ever seen a case like it?" I asked.

"Yes," said he, "I have seen several—there is no chance for him; it would have been better for him if he could not swim, as his sufferings would be sooner over. If the skipper attempted to bring the ship to the wind in this gale, and with this sea running, she'd sweep her decks, and would most likely be thrown on her beam-ends;" and he turned and went down the rigging, saying, "It's no use looking; come on to dinner, they are going to strike eight bells."

All through that afternoon, some of our comrades were fancying that they could hear the voice of the lost man astern, borne on the gale to the ship; once I thought I heard him myself, but he must have been several miles astern then, and the moaning of the wind through the rigging, the creaking of blocks and ropes, the noises made by the seas as they broke under our stern, and the strange and weird sounds familiar to the sailor, in a gale of wind, in a sailing ship at sea, were construed by them into resemblances of the human voice.

The lost man was not one of the ship's crew, but one of our volunteers, who ran aloft when the order was given, but he had been at sea before; only that morning I had been talking to him about his home and friends; he was an English lad, a native of Liverpool, where he told me his mother and sister kept a shop.

He had been an apprentice on board a Liverpool ship, and had run away in New York, and made a voyage in an American coaster before joining this expedition; he was only a year or two older than myself, and like me, he had not a single acquaintance on board the ship.

There was not much noise at dinner that day, the loss of this youth taken so suddenly from amongst us acted as a damper on every one's spirits; but before sundown, as the wind abated, and more reefs had to be shaken out to keep the ship ahead of the sea, every one seemed to forget the accident, and when the watch was set at eight bells at night, the ship was once more under all plain sail, and making ten knots an hour on her course. Such is life and death at sea; with a fair wind and fine weather, sailors soon forget their misfortunes.

It is customary when a man dies, or is lost at sea, for the captain of the ship to auction off his effects the following day for the benefit of his relations, but in this case it was not done—why, I cannot say. Perhaps the drowned man had none, or if he had, they were probably appropriated by some of the men, for there were men in our little army on board that ship from all classes of society; the off-scourings of civilisation, men from whom I shrank with loathing, whose conversation was nauseating and loathsome in the extreme. There were thieves and jail-birds amongst them; there were also ex-officers of the British Army and Navy, whose misconduct or misfortune drove them there; young men who had been educated for the Church and the Bar; youths fresh from school, and men of several callings, with a sprinkling of old soldiers.

CHAPTER II.

Barney—His story—Blackbird catching—The "Isle of Pines"
—The slaver's hidden money—Yarns.

THERE was a man with us who went by the name of Barney, a native of Troy, in the state of New York. Barney was a sailor by profession, and although still a young man, had seen a good deal of the world, as sailors see it; he was a bold, daring fellow, and often spoke to me of his voyages and adventures in various parts of the world; he was unscrupulous, and would hesitate at nothing to accomplish his ends, and yet he was not without a certain rough generosity and sense of fair play; he was a good fellow to have for a friend, for he would share his scanty clothing, or his last dollar, or risk his life and think nothing of it, to help a shipmate of only a few days' acquaintanceship, if he took a liking to him, but he was an implacable enemy. He appeared to take a liking to me from the first day he spoke to me on board the *Darthula*, and obliged and assisted me in many ways.

He was a good sailor, and taught me many things that proved of service to me in after life; he was what the men called a good yarner, and must have had a great deal of experience, or a fertile imagination, for many a night in our watch on deck on the outward passage, did a crowd of youths like myself gather round him under the lee of the long-boat, and press him to spin us a yarn, and he rarely disappointed us. For my part I must say that I listened eagerly to his stories, and was amused and interested in them, although many of them were not of a character to improve the morals or elevate the tastes of a young man.

One fine day on the voyage out, I had distinguished myself by harpooning a porpoise. I was out standing on the martingale back-ropes and supporting myself by leaning against the martingale, or dolphin striker, as it is sometimes called, just under the end of the bowsprit, with the harpoon grasped with both hands, and watching for an opportunity to throw it whenever a fish passed underneath, as the ship rose and fell with the sea, and ploughed her way through the water; at last a porpoise darted past underneath me, and I threw the harpoon with all my force, and with good aim, for I had the good fortune to strike my fish.

The line that was fast to the harpoon led up to and through a tail-block fastened at the bowsprit end, and so in onto the forecastle, and although the men on deck promptly hauled in the line, as soon as they saw that the fish was fairly struck, and soon had him dangling in the air, still he would probably have wriggled off the harpoon and made his escape, if Barney had not run out along the back-ropes with a spare line and cleverly slipped a running bowline over his tail and secured him. It was while out here, hanging over the sea, after the fish had been sent in on deck, and with our feet almost touching the water, as the ship rose and fell, while we waited for a chance to strike another fish, that Barney told me the following story.

He had been laid up with yellow fever in a hospital at New Orleans, many years ago when he was a boy; the beds in the hospital were so close together that there was barely room for a person to pass between them. One morning the occupant of one of the beds next him was found dead, and was carried out, but before night the bed was occupied by another patient, an old sailor. Barney, who was convalescent, soon discovered that his neighbour could speak several languages, for he spoke in French to the doctors, in English to Barney, and in his ravings he sometimes spoke in Spanish or Portuguese; in his lucid moments he "spun many a yarn" to Barney of his voyages, and about "blackbird catching." Here Barney explained to me that blackbird catching meant slaving.

The old sailor said that he had spent twenty years

of his life in the slave trade, and had been part-owner of schooners in that trade at one time, and had made several successful trips, but that very often, after running a cargo, they had to destroy the vessel, but even then they always made money; the slaves were landed either in Cuba or Brazil. He had run two cargoes to the Brazilian coast, and after landing the mokes, as he called the slaves, he was obliged to burn the vessel. The last run that he made was in a vessel built by himself, with the assistance of a few men; they built a schooner of a hundred and twenty tons, out of green timber cut in the woods by themselves. She was sparred and rigged with materials procured from two old wrecks on the coast; even the bolts and fastenings were obtained from the same source, and fashioned by themselves to the shape and size required. She was caulked to the water-line with oakum made from some old rigging, and above that with a fibrous plant found near the Cuban creeks; canvas was the only material that they had to buy, and they cut and made the sails themselves. The running rigging was made from green cow-hide, and the little vessel was built, launched, manned, equipped, and sailed from a lone and unfrequented part of the coast of Cuba for the African coast, where she took in a load of slaves, and despite the cruisers of various European nations, made the run safely across the Atlantic and landed them in Brazil; but she was chased on the Brazilian coast, and had to be run ashore and set on fire to avoid capture. The crew compelled the slaves to jump overboard and swim ashore; the old man, who was captain of the schooner, was detained by the Brazilian authorities for over six months, and at last, when set at liberty, he discovered that his officers and crew, who he admitted were his partners and part-owners of the vessel, had disappeared with the proceeds of the sale of the slaves, and left him without means of any kind. He was so reduced that he was obliged to beg on the streets of Rio Janeiro; for as he was old no one cared to employ him, and he only understood such work as sailors are employed at, and his ragged and broken-down appearance was against him; he could not get employment, and was glad to accept a milreis or an odd dollar now and again from sailors he met on shore on liberty; he never asked or obtained assistance from any one but sailors, men of his own calling.

He had been living this wretched, miserable life in Rio for months, when at last he fell in with a man who had been a shipmate of his years before, and through him he got a chance to work his way on board a vessel to New Orleans, from which port he hoped to make his way to Cuba; but he had not been many days there before he was stricken with yellow fever and brought to the hospital, where he then lay, without a cent in his pocket or a coat on his back, and "Here I am," said he, "dying a pauper, whereas if I were only in a spot I know well in the island of Cuba, I would be worth thousands of dollars to-day."

He told Barney that he had hidden away the profits of two former voyages, both his own and the men's share. He said: "We put it away the day before we sailed, in the presence of all hands; but at night I got my cook, a mulatto, to assist me, and between us we shifted the money to another place that I had determined on some time before, having already marked it out and taken its bearings, so that I could easily find it again. The cook I managed to leave on the coast of Africa, and I don't think he'll ever come back, so that no one knows where the money is hid but myself. If my late crew and partners go back to look for it they'll be disappointed, and will think some one else discovered the money and took it away. They would never suspect me, as they left me behind them in prison in Rio, but I am to windward of them. It matters little now, I shall never get back. I am done for, and can't last much longer."

On another occasion when Barney was speaking to him, telling him to cheer up and get better, and he would go with him to Cuba and help him to recover the money, he said: "No, my lad, if I were to get better I wouldn't want your assistance. My line is about played out, and I'll soon slip my cable, for I'll never leave this hospital alive. But I may as well do you a good turn as any one else, for there isn't one in the world that I care a —— about."

He gave Barney a rough chart of a part of the coast of the "Isle of Pines," an island about twenty leagues off the south-west coast of Cuba, and told him that if he ever got there he could, by the aid of that chart, easily find where the money was buried, for the bearings and distances were all carefully marked and noted on it, and if he followed out the instructions there given he could not fail to find it.

The old man died, and Barney left the hospital completely recovered a few days afterwards.

"Now," said Barney, "I've carried that chart for years about with me. When I left the hospital I went round to Boston in a fore-and-after, and—to tell the truth—I didn't think there was much in the old slaver's yarn. I believed he was an old fraud, but I kept his chart all the time. I thought there might be a chance of making a few dollars out of it by spinning a long yarn about it, and selling it to some fool or other with more money than sense. Anyhow, I had no money, and I thought I'd ship for a long voyage somewhere, and, when I got back to the States with a few dollars, if I could pick up a good chum, we'd look out for a West Indiaman bound for Cuba, and try and ship in her, and leave her there and make for the Isle of Pines, and see if there was anything in the old pirate's yarn. If there wasn't—why, we'd be no worse off than we were before; so I shipped in a large, full-rigged ship bound for Melbourne, Australia, but we were treated so badly on board by the skipper and the mates on the passage out, that the whole crew ran away from her in Melbourne. I went up to the diggin's at Ballarat, and fell in with some new chums there, as I told you before," alluding to some stories he had told us in the dog-watches a few nights before about the gold-diggings; going to new rushes; getting stuck-up; walking to Sydney; going to sea again and trading with the South Sea islands some of which would fill a book. "Well, chum," he continued, "when I found myself in New York this time, and heard of this craft, and that they wanted men for Cuba, I determined to be in it. Now what do you think I joined this expedition for?"

"Well," I replied, "I suppose you joined like the rest of us, to liberate the Cubans and to see the world; and maybe with an eye to bettering your position and prospects."

"No, chum, I don't care two copper cents if the expedition and the Cubans were all at the bottom of the sea, if I can only get to the 'Isle of Pines.' I've got the old chart with me here on board, and I'm bound to have the old slaver's spondulix this time, if they're there. You can bet your bottom dollar on that." Then after a pause, and looking me straight in the face: "What do you say? Will you come? We'll go shares in the money or whatever we find."

"But, Barney," I said, "we would be deserters and traitors to the expedition."

"Oh," said Barney, "I see you're green yet. How much did you get for coming on board here?"

"Nothing," I replied, "but my arms, uniform, shirt, trousers, hat, and blanket."

"I wa'n't such a darned fool as that," said Barney. "I got thirty dollars advance from them, and they had to pay twenty-five I owed at a boarding-house before they yanked me on board; although I'd made up my mind to come, any way, I wa'n't going to let them best me if I knew it. Do you know how this business is run?"

I confessed my ignorance, and Barney undertook to enlighten me.

"The people in New York who fitted out this vessel care about as much for Cuban independence as I do, and that's to make as many dollars as they can out of it. As long as the Cubans can raise the spondulix, they'll get plenty of people to fit out expeditions for them. For every man on board this craft you can bet your boots they don't get less than a hundred dollars; and then the provisions, arms, ammunition, and shoddy uniforms and blankets that they serve out are old Government stores, condemned, very likely, and bought up cheaply to be sold to the Cubans at the biggest prices. The ship they charter at twice her value, because she runs the risk of capture, although, most likely, the chances are that she cleared at New York Custom House for some of the West India islands; and when she lands *this* crowd in Cuba, she'll slink away to Turk's Island for a load of salt, and away home as innocent as if she'd never been anywhere else, and they'll have her to the good again, after making their pile out of her and a lot of greenhorns like you."

" But what about the officers, Barney ? " I asked.

"Wal—if they've not got something worth while'—speaking very slowly—"or their eye on some other game—wal, they're greater darned fools than I take them to be, that's all I say."

As the porpoises had all disappeared, and we had been a long time out under the jibboom while we were spinning this yarn, I fastened the harpoon to the martingale, and making a neat coil of the harpoon line, and securing it to the jib-stay, I followed Barney in on deck, remarking as we climbed in by the bowsprit :

" Why didn't you keep that yarn till night, Barney, and tell it to the watch ? "

"No, chum, there's no yarn about *that*, as sure as you're born. Look here! Don't you say anything to anybody about it. I want you to keep it to yourself—eh?"

"Oh, all right, if it's a secret."

"I'll show you the chart one of these days when we get a chance of being alone, and you'll find it's all square and jonick."

"Very good."

CHAPTER III.

Arrival on the coast of Cuba—Chased by a war steamer—Short of coal—Run for the Mosquito coast—Wood-cutting—March inland—An Indian village and women—Polygamy and Polyandry.

AFTER a voyage of about three weeks with varying winds and weather, and, to me, some strange and new experiences, the ship arrived off the coast of Cuba, and cruised along it, watching for signals, or an opportunity of communicating with our friends on shore.

The fires were lit and steam got up on the boilers, and we steamed close in-shore and kept signals flying from the mast-heads all day to no purpose; it was not until the following day about noon that a signal was seen and answered, and we steamed in and prepared to anchor, but before we could effect our purpose, a Spanish war steamer was seen steering for us, and we stood out to sea again under all sail and steam, the Spaniard following in pursuit. He must have seen the signals made to us from the shore and divined their meaning, for he followed us up persistently all that afternoon, and as the night was clear moonlight he kept up the chase, for we could see his smoke still in our wake ; but at daylight he was nowhere to be seen, and as our supply of coal was running short, for we used more than was intended on the passage out, and it would never do to run short if we were chased by the enemy, we shaped a course for the Mosquito Coast, on the mainland of Central America, to replenish our stock of fuel. Our fires were let die out and we proceeded under sail.

A few nights after this, the ship being under all plain sail, in the early part of the first watch, or from eight to twelve at night, I was on deck; a good topgallant breeze was blowing at the time, and with the wind abeam the ship struck the bottom, lifted, and as she fell in the trough of the sea, struck again. Here, I thought, is the end of our voyage; we were on a sunk reef with no land in sight, and with the breeze that was blowing she would soon knock herself to pieces. She bumped four or five times before she got clear; the water was very shallow, and the bank we struck on must have been mud. The same thing happened an hour afterwards, and then we got into deeper water. The captain was on deck when this happened, but no alteration was made in the trim of the ship, no order given to shorten sail or alter the

WE SIGHT THE MAINLAND.

course; and that partly reassured me that there was nothing seriously wrong, but when the pump-well was sounded it was discovered that she was making a little water. The knocking must have shaken her a good deal, although it was on a mud-bank, for she had to be pumped out regularly every two hours, night and day afterwards, all the time we remained on board of her. Hitherto she had been as tight as a drum, and had never once been pumped out since leaving New York, even in bad weather.

After a week's sailing we sighted the mainland of Central America, and ran down the coast until we found a suitable place, where we anchored off the mouth of a small river. A boat was lowered and sent with five men and an officer to take soundings; they found that there was a bar across the mouth of the river, with only a few feet of water on it, and no possibility of the ship being able to get in; otherwise the place was suitable enough, for there seemed to be an abundance of wood to be had for the cutting. As we were not likely to find a better place on the coast, and we would have to remain outside at anchor on an exposed coast in any case, it was decided to remain there and proceed with all despatch to cut and load the wood.

Early the following morning all hands were busy in preparing the boats; tackles were got up on the fore and main yardarms to hoist out the launch, the largest and heaviest boat in the ship, and in a surprisingly short time every boat in the ship was hoisted out and alongside, and the men were stowing arms, axes, cross-cut saws, grindstones, provisions, tents, and a ship's awning in them. All this work was finished before seven, and after an early breakfast fifty men started for the shore in the boats. We were soon across the bar and pulling up-stream.

Looking from on board the ship, there appeared to be plenty of good timber close at hand, but we found when we entered the river that the trees most suitable for us were rather far apart, and we had to pull further up the river. We landed several times without being able to find a place to our liking; and we had to go about three miles up before we found a suitable place for wood-cutting.

It was well on in the afternoon before we disembarked. We took everything out of the boats and proceeded at once to form an encampment; three parties of ten men and an officer were sent out in three different directions to reconnoitre, while the remainder fixed the tents and awning, cleared a place round the encampment, and prepared supper.

The party to which I was attached started in a north-west direction for about two miles, without seeing any natives or signs of a habitation, and then returned; we had to cut a path in some places for ourselves in going, and as we did not return by the same path, but made a slight detour, we often had to open a road with axe and sabre on our return; we were told not to fire a shot or do anything to alarm the natives if it could be avoided.

It was night when we got back to the encampment, and found that the other two parties had returned like ours, without finding any trace of Indians. A guard was set for the night, and sentries posted round the camp and relieved every two hours until daylight.

In the morning the boats were sent back to the ship for more men, to enable us to get through quickly with the wood-cutting, and all hands and all the men were put to work to fell trees, and cut up and pile the wood ready for loading in the boats; six sentries were posted around the wood-cutters.

That afternoon one of the sentries reported that he had seen two Indians watching him, but when he called to them they disappeared; so when the boats returned from the ship about sundown with over forty additional men, it was decided to send out a party next morning to look for them, and try and procure fresh meat of some kind.

I had worked hard all day cutting wood, the hardest wood I had ever seen, and my hands not being accustomed to such work, were covered with blisters; and as I was not able to do much at wood-cutting, I was detailed one of the exploring party.

We started early in the morning, our party consisting of twenty men and two officers, taking our arms blankets, and two days' rations with us, and some hand-rockets to signal our whereabouts to the encampment, in case we should lose our way. We marched all day towards the interior, following the course of the river up-stream, and keeping near it for the sake of the water, and also with the hope of falling in with some Indian canoes. A halt was made about eleven in the forenoon for breakfast; that consisted of a ship's biscuit and a slice of cold salt pork, washed down with a drink of water from the river; as the pork was simply a lump of fat, without any lean meat on it, and as I never could manage to swallow grease, my breakfast was simply a biscuit and a drink of water.

After a two hours' rest we resumed our march, one of the men having first climbed a tree to ascertain the trend of the river, and then we struck inland, intending to make the river again higher up before nightfall, but we filled our water-cans, as a precaution, in the event of not being able to do so; to our great surprise, in about two hours' time we found ourselves near the river again, but could not reach it for the dense growth of bush and bamboo; a little further on we heard the water rushing over stones in some shallow place, and shortly after we emerged on a comparatively open space, where, with a slight effort,

AN INDIAN VILLAGE.

we managed to open a way through the bamboo to a little sandy beach, and disturbed some half-dozen alligators that were basking in the sun.

The only animals that we had seen since we left the encampment were monkeys and carpinchos. The river got very narrow here, and as we advanced further it was completely arched over by the trees on each side, and presented the appearance of a cave, with a stream of water flowing out of it; a little further on again it narrowed to not more than five or six yards in width, where it rushed between precipitous rocks. We had to wade through the water to get past, the water reaching our breasts in some places, and we were obliged to hold our arms, ammunition, and rations above our heads to keep them dry, and even with this weight we had to go cautiously to avoid being washed off our feet, the current was so strong in the narrow places. After getting through this gorge the country became more open, and the land higher, but we still kept by the river. In our eagerness to get ahead we had almost overlooked a narrow pathway which led from the river into the forest—in fact, it was an iguana pursued by one of the men that guided us to it; by following this pathway we came on a collection of Indian huts, or village, occupied by women and children; there were only two old men in the place, while there appeared to be about forty women, and almost as many children. They did not seem at all alarmed at our intrusion, and as one of the old men understood a little Spanish, we were able to converse with them; they gave us to understand that the men of the village were on the sea-coast somewhere, engaged in turtle-fishing.

The children were shy at first on seeing us, but after awhile made their appearance, and stared at us from behind the trees and huts; the women wore nothing more than a coarse cloth, or a piece of matting, round their hips. I only saw one woman with a short chemise, and there did not appear to be any old women among them; the boys and girls of all ages went quite naked, and only seemed to think of decorating their heads with feathers and pieces of bone and wood.

These people were kindly and hospitable, and seemed anxious to propitiate us, but at the same time to get all they could out of us; and they understood well how to drive a bargain, and put a good price on anything they had to sell. They were very dirty in their habits, and it would appear that both polygamy and polyandry are practised among them, as the following incident tended to show.

I observed two rather pretty children, a boy and a girl about four and five years of age, watching me, and by offering them a biscuit from my haversack, which they eagerly accepted, I managed to make

AN OFFER OF MARRIAGE. 31

friends with them. They walked round me and examined my rifle and sabre, and would have explored the inside of my haversack if I had not used a little gentle persuasion to prevent them.

While I was busy with the children an Indian woman came forward, and laying a hand on my arm, spoke to me and pointed to the children. When she saw that I could not understand a word of what she said, she went and brought one of the old men, who spoke a little Spanish, to talk to me, but I was as badly off as ever, for I did not understand Spanish at that time, and I had to ask one of our officers who spoke Spanish to act as interpreter for me. The woman told me that she was the mother of the children to whom I had given the biscuit, and proposed to become my wife while I remained there. I am not quite sure whether it was with the contents of my haversack or with myself that she fell in love. The lieutenant chaffed me on my conquest of the dusky widow and her two children, but I asked: "How did her husband die?" And then we were given to understand that her husband was not dead, but absent down the coast, and would not return for some time; that even if he did come back it would not matter much, as he had two other wives. I excused myself by telling her that I could not take a wife without the permission of my chief, and by presenting her with what pork was in my haversack and half a biscuit, I effectually soothed her wounded feelings.

None of these women had pretty faces, according to European ideas of prettiness, but there were several of them beautifully formed, and on the whole they might be called beautiful if they were only cleanly in their habits, but it was a beauty that appealed only to the senses. The poor creatures had small clearings or plantations, near their huts, where they—the women, for the men never work at planting—cultivated, after a fashion, maize, beans, and yams. They had some monkeys and parrots domesticated, but I did not see either a dog or a cat. They cooked some iguanas—a large lizard, some of them four and five feet long—and offered them to us with roasted yams and maize, and most of our men ate them and described them as delicious, something like chicken; but I did not try them. I could not overcome my repugnance to the reptile, and contented myself with the yams and the maize.

As night came on, we looked about for a suitable place to camp on. The Indians kindly offered us their huts, but one look at them was sufficient; they were disgustingly dirty, and we declined the offer. Nevertheless, they brought out grass hammocks and slung them between the trees for us.

The mosquitoes were as bad here as at the encampment, and the Indians, who go naked, must suffer very much from them. I could only get to sleep by covering myself with my blanket, leaving only a small opening to breathe through, and although I perspired profusely from being so closely covered up, still it was less distressing than the annoyance from the mosquitoes.

In the morning our officers had another conference with the two old men, and we learned that we would have to make a three days' march from where we were before we could find cattle, and as it would take at least as many more to return, and we could not spare that time unless we wished to abandon the ship, for she would have sailed before that time, it was decided to return to the encampment. We failed to find out from the old men if they were the two Indians seen by our sentries near the encampment. They either could not or would not understand us when questioned on the subject.

After an early breakfast we prepared to return to the wood-cutting encampment, and several of the Indian women accompanied us loaded with yams, sweet potatoes, green plantains, and bananas, which they wished to exchange for pork and biscuit. On our way back we saw several iguanas on the branches of the trees overhanging the river, and the Indian women, and even the children, showed great dexterity in shooting them with bows and arrows. As they often dropped into the river when shot, the Indians, without a moment's hesitation, rushed into the water after them without any fear of the alligators with which it was infested.

We halted at noon for a rest, and made fires to cook a midday meal, and drive away the mosquitoes with the smoke, for even in the day-time we found them very troublesome under the trees. The women cooked the iguanas that they killed in the forenoon. The flesh looked white and nice, but still I could not overcome my repugnance, and I again contented myself with a vegetable diet.

We got a good many hints from the Indians, in the matter of cookery, that were of service to us afterwards. We learned from them that plantains and bananas could be boiled and roasted when green, and we often had to content ourselves with them prepared in that manner in Cuba. After a short siesta we started again on the march, the women carrying the loads, and very heavy loads some of them had to carry, as many of them had young children with them, and carried them sitting astride their hip, on one side, in the same fashion as their southern sisters in Paraguay carry theirs, or the Hindoo women in India. I offered to lighten the load of one woman by carrying her child, for she would not let me carry her plantains, but all the others laughed at me, and called me a woman, and finally the woman to whom the child belonged came and snatched it from me, and would not allow me to carry it. We reached the encampment before night, and after a hearty supper of roast parrakeets and wood-pigeon, we lay down to fight the mosquitoes and sleep if we could.

CHAPTER IV.

Barney—His story—Tempted to desert—Barney's plan—His idea of happiness.

THE morning after our arrival in the encampment from the Indian village, we were kept busy getting the wood loaded in the boats, and ready to take to the ship. None of the ship's crew were on shore with us, and my friend Barney, who was well known to every one as a good sailor, was told by one of our officers to pick out such of our men as had been at sea, or knew how to handle a boat, and place them as boat's crews, and take the wood off to the ship. Barney appointed himself and three others to the launch, and called to me, saying:

"You can pull an oar, can't you, or steer?"

And when I said "Yes, I can do either,"

"Well, then, jump in the launch and take the tiller. I'll pull the stroke oar myself; as you're a young lad you can steer."

The launch, or long-boat, was the largest boat

the ship had, and was fitted with a canvas cover, and had a mast and sails and four small water-breakers or little barrels for holding water, in her for ballast; loaded up as she was with wood to go off to the ship the sails were not used, but they were in the boat, rolled up and stowed away under the thwarts. When everything was ready we started down the river; the two quarter-boats were ahead, and the launch brought up the rear; the men in the encampment meanwhile were occupied in cutting wood and bringing it down to the bank of the river, ready for loading in the boats. We had gone about a mile down the stream, and the other boats were a good way ahead of us, when Barney rested a while on his oar, and said to us:

"Now look here, boys. Easy a moment with your oars," and looking over his shoulder ahead at the other boats, "Let them other boats get round the bend. That's all right," and lifting his oar out of the water, and holding it by throwing one leg over it and holding it under his knee, he put his hand in the breast of his shirt, and drew out a paper, which proved to be the chart the old slaver had given him of the Isle of Pines, about which he had told me so much on the passage out, and laying his finger on it, said:

"There's the spot where the old slaver's dollars are stowed away. I spoke to ye all before about it, and I've thought the thing over a good deal since, and come to the conclusion that we couldn't have a better chance than this. Look here, chum," addressing me, "drop the tiller and come here; the boat is all right, she'll drift down with the current. Come and look at this. This is the chart I told you about, and here is another," said he, producing a piece of a Central American chart. "Here is the Nicaraguan, or Mosquito Coast, where we are just now; this is Cape Gracias a Dios, the landfall we made, don't you remember, last week, when we came on the coast. We're south of it, somewhere here," laying his finger on the chart; "how much I can't say, but certainly not a hundred miles. These three chaps here," nodding his head towards the other men in the boat, "are all good sailors. I've spoken to them, and they're willing to go; and between us five fellows, it will be hard lines if we don't root out the spondulix—if they're there; and if they're not—why, we lose nothing, but perhaps save our throats from being cut, which we stand a good chance of if we remain in this hooker. For look you, if the Spaniards capture this vessel they'll hang or cut the weasands of every Jack-man aboard." And rolling up his papers, he replaced them in his breast, and continued: "Now, what I propose to do is this. When we get alongside the ship this trip, and get the wood on board, I'll look round for anything that I see and think might be useful to us, and watch a chance to drop it into the boat, and one of you be on the lookout to stow it away; and when we go ashore again for another load, while loading the boat we can stow away a good many things in the boat's locker and the sternsheets that may come in handy afterwards. Now, give way, boys, give way and pull a stroke; don't let us be too far behind the other boats."

As soon as they began pulling again, he resumed:

"Wal, as I was saying, we must have all prepared for the last trip to-morrow evening, and contrive to be behind the other boats on the last trip, and as soon as we get them out of sight in one of those bends we'll run the boat in among the mangrove bushes, and pitch the wood overboard and hide the boat there till dark, and then pull up quietly past the encampment, and go up the river as high as we can and hide the boat again there, and walk on to the Indian village. You've been there, and can guide us," he said, addressing me. "Once there, we can lay back and take things easy until the ship is gone off the coast. They'll never think of looking for us in the river, but will conclude that we've gone along the coast. But if they should search for us here we must get the Indians to bamboozle them, and let us know when the ship is gone. Once the ship is away we can get a lot of yams and bananas into the boat, and fill the water breakers with fresh water, and go to sea, and head north along the coast. When we get round Cape Gracias a Dios, I've been told that it's a splendid country, and we can land every night if we like, or whenever we want provisions."

" That's all very well, Barney," I replied; " but we must be a long way from the Isle of Pines here. Why, we were nearly a week coming from the coast of Cuba in the ship."

" Don't you fret yourself, chum," said Barney; " I've worked out the hull thing. It's seven hundred and fifty miles from Cape Gracias a Dios to the island of Cosumel, on the coast of Yutacan, sailing along the coast, and from Cosumel across to the Isle of Pines is only two hundred and fifty, or a thousand miles altogether, and I'll eat my boots if this boat can't make forty miles a day. Why, we'd get there within a month, fine weather all the time. We needn't be out of sight of land except for the few days crossing over from one island to the other. The longest part of the journey will be along the coast, and if we see any sign of dirty weather at any time we can up helm and run ashore till it blows over. We're our own masters, there's no one to hurry us; no rousing out in the middle watch of a dirty night to reef topsails. Eh, boys?" said he, looking over his shoulder at the other three men.

" That's so, Barney," they answered.

As I made no reply to this he continued addressing himself to me:

"There's no hurry about it, chum, if you wish. In fact, I think myself that it would be better to wait a week or so after the ship sails before making a move, so as to allow her time to search along the coast for us if she felt inclined to do so."

"But suppose, Barney, that when they missed us they sent a party to the Indian village to make inquiries, and offer a reward for us; and suppose we were caught, we should never get another chance to leave, even on the coast of Cuba; we'd be looked after so closely. You didn't think of that, did you?"

"Yes, chum, I've thought of that, and I've picked up enough Spanish when I was in Manilla to be able to spin the Indians a yarn. We'll tell them that as soon as the ship sails we're expecting another ship with our friends, and loaded chock-a-block with pork and biscuits, and fancy dresses, and that we'll give them all they want if they don't split on us."

"Well, admitting that they don't find us, but find the boat, which they would be sure to do if they came up the river and made a thorough search. What then, Barney? We would be marooning ourselves for nothing here on the Mosquito Coast, amongst a tribe of savages, and I don't see where you're going to make anything by that, or where the fun of it comes in."

Barney was silent for a few moments, and then suddenly stopped pulling, and, slapping one leg with his hand, said :

"I've got it! Look here, chum, you say that there were no men up at the Indian village but two old fellows, and that the others were down the coast turtle-fishing. Well, I reckon they've got some kind of craft to float on, if they're only dug-outs; and supposen the ship does find the launch, they won't best us, for we can lay back at the village until the Indians return with their dug-outs, and we can make a good, comfortable sea boat—at least, good enough for these seas—by lashing two or three of them together; and it won't be the first time that I've been to sea in a dug-out. And that just reminds me that we must get hold of the carpenter's tools if we can ;" and looking round he asked the other men, " Do any of you fellows know where ' Chips ' keeps his nails ? "

"I know where there are a lot of scupper nails," said one, "and some pump tack."

" When we get alongside, you jump up on deck and get them, and any augers or chisels you find lying about," said Barney; " axes we needn't bother about, we can get plenty of them and cross-cut saws ashore at the encampment, but a hand-saw and an adze or two would come in very handy; and if ' Chips ' has them locked up we must spin him a yarn that Captain Ryan wants the lend of them ashore; but to-morrow will be time enough for that."

"But how do you know that the Indians will let you take their dug-outs?" I asked.

"I ain't going to take them, chum; I'm going to buy them from the Indians."

"Buy them!" I asked with astonishment. "With what?"

"Why, for an axe or a saw, I guess I can buy a dug-out from these Indians, or they ain't what I take them to be; and if all comes to all, why shouldn't we five fellows, with some carpenter's tools, and the help of the Indians, be able to knock up some kind of a craft good enough for coasting along here, and running across to the Isle of Pines? If the old slaver and his half-a-dozen of a crew could build, launch, and rig a hundred-and-twenty-ton schooner, I don't see why we shouldn't be able to fix up a craft of some kind; but I don't think there'll be any necessity for it—although it's well to be prepared for everything—for if they find the boat after I've hidden her, then I'm a Dutchman."

Barney saw that I hesitated, and used every argument that he could think of to persuade me, and I for my part could see that it would be useless to appeal to his sense of loyalty to the expedition, after the opinion he expressed regarding it, and I did not attempt it; but I suggested that it would be better to wait until the ship reached Cuba, than run the risk of a long and dangerous coasting voyage in an open boat.

"No," said he, "we will never get such another chance as this; it's right into our hand. What better chance could you wish for? For let me tell you, that when the ship gets to Cuba this time—if ever she does get there, for she runs a good chance of capture —the men and arms will be bundled ashore anyhow; as long as they get them out of her, that's all they care about; and the hull lot will be landed in an hour or two, and marched right away inland, and the ship will clear out as quickly as wind and steam can take her off the coast; and then where would our chance be if we go with her? No, chum, this is a ripping chance that we mustn't let slide."

Leaving me to think over it, they bent themselves to their oars, and we were soon alongside the ship. Barney and one of the boat's crew went on deck with the intention of picking up some of the carpenter's tools, or anything else that would be useful, as they declared in coming off, while I remained in the boat with the other two to unload the wood. They were only partially successful; they brought some nails into the boat, but they did not pick up any of the carpenter's tools.

We made two trips that day between the ship and

the shore, and as I did not ask any more questions, or speak any more on the subject, Barney took it for granted that I had made up my mind to go with him and his companions, and that I was only undecided as to the time and way of going.

He could not imagine for a moment that I would refuse such an opportunity of enriching myself, and no doubt considered that he was conferring a favour on me which any one on board would be pleased to accept.

I was now in great perplexity as to what I had better do. I had an idea that it was my duty to inform the officers in charge of the expedition of the intention of these men to desert and steal the boat, but on the other hand I thought that by doing so I would be betraying confidence. It is true I did not seek their confidence, it was offered to me; but then I encouraged it by listening to and entertaining their project.

I hesitated. I did not know what to do. The prospect opened up to me by Barney's proposal was very alluring. Here was an opportunity of seeing the whole Central American coast and people, such as, perhaps, would never again occur in a lifetime; of cruising along its shores, and visiting every bay and inlet, as Columbus did nearly four centuries ago, when he tried to find a passage west to China and India; of seeing the countries and people as he saw them, for the Indians of the present day have changed little, if anything, since his day. They are the same people, neither better nor worse. Here was a chance of seeing all this; of going into and exploring every creek and river as Columbus did, and in a smaller vessel even than he had, and finally ending my voyage and finding a fortune where the adventurous navigator found a grave, in the "Pearl of the Antilles," Cuba.

Perhaps this would be better than any fame I would be likely to win as a soldier in what some people called a filibustering expedition; but there was the stealing of the arms and the boat—for although the ship carried four other boats, the launch which we had was the largest, and the loss of that boat might cripple the expedition by delaying the landing, and give time to some Spanish cruiser to come up and destroy it.

I brooded all day over this proposal as I sat silently, tiller in hand, steering the boat. Barney and the rest of the boat's crew seemed to be in the best of good-humour at the thought of being soon freed from all restraint. They amused each other while pulling off to the ship and back to the shore by telling stories of former voyages, and making guesses as to the amount of money that they would find at the Isle of Pines, and as to how they would get it away, and where they would go to spend it. One of them said:

"There may be only four or five thousand dollars there after all; scarce enough to give us a thousand apiece, and that wouldn't be much."

"Why, I've known fellows come off a whaling voyage at New Bedford and have as much as that to take," said another.

"I like to hear you fellows talking," said Barney. "Now, do you think that that old slaver would be such a darned old idiot as to go and make all that fuss and trouble for the sake of a trifle of four or five thousand dollars? No, mates, you can bet your bottom dollar that there's half a million in it if there's a red cent, and the chances are that there's a pile of other stuff hidden there as well as money."

"I hope it's all money," said the other, "or something that can be easily stowed away."

"Hang the odds!" said Barney. "We've a good boat and can load her up; and if we can go from here to the Isle of Pines in her, we can surely run across from the Cuban coast to Florida. Why, it wouldn't be more than a week's run, and there's plenty of islands, or cays, that we could land on at any time. Once I got ashore in any part of the States I'd be all hunky dory."

Barney's idea was to get back to New York as quickly as possible, and take passage in some vessel sailing for San Francisco, or as he called it, "Frisco."

"A cabin passage, mind you," said he. "I'd go like a gentleman, and get the skipper to teach me navigation on the passage out—at least, all the navigation I'd care to know. I wouldn't bother much with great circle sailing, or lunars, and the likes, but just pick up enough for my purpose; plane sailing would be good enough for me. When I get to Frisco, if I can't pick up what I want there, I'll take a run up the coast to Puget Sound, in British Columbia. I know a place there where they turn out some ripping schooners cheaply, and I'd invest in a two-hundred-ton 'fore-and-after,' and bring her down to Frisco and freight her for the South Seas. Ah, boys, that's a staving place to live! Have any of you ever been there?"

"No."

"Well, I have. I've been at a good many of the islands when I sailed out of Sydney. We used to trade with them, but there are hundreds of islands without a living soul on them; beautiful islands, every one of them like a garden, covered with all kinds of trees, cocoanut trees, bread-fruit trees, banana bushes, and anything you like to mention; and as for growing, you need only make a hole with a stick and shove anything in, and 'twill grow splendidly. And for meat, why, on some of the islands there's any God's quantity of hogs running wild; and inside the coral reefs you can get all the fish you've a mind to. A white man could live like a king there if he had a schooner of his own. If ever I get there I'll look out for a good island, and then make a trip to Sydney and take in anything I wanted, and start back for the island and build a staving good house with a billiard-table, a good chum, and everything right up to the knocker. Perhaps I'd sell the schooner, and perhaps not. I'd see. I might trade from island to island, or from the islands to Sydney. Put a captain on board and live ashore myself, and get married, if all went well and jonick."

In conversation such as this they passed the time and amused themselves, each man relating his experiences and giving his ideas of things in general, and the way he intended to dispose of his share of the money when he got it.

I expected every moment to be challenged by one of them, and asked what I intended doing with my share, but they were too busy thinking on their own plans, and left me alone to my thoughts.

CHAPTER V.

My first smoke—Barney's plan frustrated—We sail again—Blewfields—Sick—Attempt to land at Cuba—Chased by a war brig—Under fire—Threatened mutiny—Boat shot away.

THE mosquitoes were very bad at the encampment that night, and I was recommended to try tobacco smoking to keep them off my face. One of the men lent me a pipe and some tobacco, and I tried smoking for the first time, and smoked until I made myself sick, but to very little purpose, until the air cooled down about midnight, when we got a little relief from these pests. My companions dropped off to sleep one by one, and left me awake and alone. I could not sleep with thinking: what should I do? I must decide before morning, for probably all the wood would be on board the next day, and the day following the ship would sail.

If I were to go with these men, and if we succeeded in reaching the Isle of Pines, and discovering where the old slaver had hidden his money,

WHAT SHOULD I DO? 51

and divided it, each man getting an equal share, I would be able to get back home with a large sum of money in a few months, instead of having to suffer toil and hardship, and risk life and limb for years in the pursuit of fame and fortune that might never reach me. In reality, the chance of roving adventure offered by Barney's proposal had more attraction for me than the slaver's money, although that was always something to look forward to as an agreeable ending to our cruise : the prize money to be obtained for our risks and hardships in the open boat. But then again, I had pledged myself to fight for the independence of Cuba, and never to lay down my arms until the end of the campaign, or until discharged. I was a Cuban soldier fairly enlisted, and understood all the risks and responsibilities of the position before I accepted it; and yet, here I was, without ever landing on its shores or striking a blow for its people, planning a desertion and about to become a traitor and a swindler, merely to gratify a caprice or for the sordid purpose of searching for money, the price of human flesh and blood.

Again I thought, I will persuade Barney to relinquish his intention of going to look for the money until the end of the campaign, and the independence of Cuba is secured, then we could go freely and openly; but a moment's reflection convinced me that he would only laugh at me. Besides, I felt in my own mind that Cuban independence was very problematical indeed if it depended on our expedition; and although I was willing to risk my life for it, I was old enough to know that in expeditions such as ours, success was oftener the exception than the rule, and that in any event many on board our ship would be gone to the great unknown long before the final success could be obtained. Still there was a chance of success, and the greater the risk the greater the honour, and the more glorious the victory.

The struggle within me was hard. Inclination pulled me one way, while duty pointed the other. At last, about an hour before daylight, I got up, decided that it was my duty to prevent the desertion. I had made no promise of secrecy to Barney, yet I did not like to get him into trouble. I went to where the captain of my company slept, and quietly woke him up, and after exacting from him a promise that Barney would not be punished, I disclosed the whole plan. He thanked me, and promised that he would arrange everything without compromising me or leading the others to suspect that their intention was known, and told me to go in the boat as usual in the morning and leave everything else to him. I then went and lay down again, and slept so soundly that Barney had to come and wake me up to go in the boat at daylight. I found everybody working with a will as if anxious to get away, and we soon had the boat loaded and ready to start for the ship. Barney upbraided me for sleeping so long in the morning. He said:

"If you had been up, like the rest of us, before any one in the camp was moving, you could have smuggled your arms into the boat without any of the officers seeing you. See, we've got a lot of biscuit and pork. I stole it last night from the cook, besides our rifles, while you did nothing but sleep. Sleep! Now is the time for work, chum. When we get away you can sleep for a week if you've a mind to, but you must look spry just now, and keep your eye lifting for anything you can pick up. If we work hard we can make four trips to-day, and that will leave us pretty late in the evening on the last trip, and bring us in nicely, and you"—addressing himself particularly to me—"must look out for a chance and get your rifle in the boat before we shove off for the last trip in the evening."

We worked so well that we were the first boat alongside the ship that morning, and while we were discharging the wood, I noticed that my captain came off in one of the other boats, and going on deck, he soon after appeared at the gangway with the captain of the ship, and entered into a conversation with him, looking over the side and speaking loud enough for the men in the boats to hear him.

Our captain asked the captain of the ship:

"How many more boatloads of wood can you find room for on board here?"

"For all your men can bring on board to-day, I dare say," replied the ship's captain. "But if the boats are well loaded and kept going all day, I guess by sundown we'll have all we require on board. But look here"—apparently noting the boat's sails and masts for the first time, as he looked over the side into the boat—"what in thunder do you men carry that boat's mast and sails for backwards and forwards every trip? You can make no use of them, and they are only lumbering up the boat. Look here, you can stow twice as much wood in that launch as you're doing if you clean her out properly. Pass up that mast and sail here on deck. I thought these men of yours were sailors, Captain Ryan!"

And calling the second mate of the ship, he told him to go down into the boat and see that she was cleared out properly.

"You want nothing in that boat," he said, "but a man to steer; then you can load her right up, and tow her off with any of the smaller boats."

Everything was handed up on deck out of the boat: sails, mast, oars, water breakers, the canvas cover that was rolled up and shoved away in the bow, our rifles, or rather those of Barney and his three companions, all the biscuit and pork that he took such trouble to steal from the cook; the second mate found the scupper nails and pump tack; in fact, the boat was thoroughly cleared out, and nothing left in her but the tiller. As the provisions were handed up the captain simply remarked:

"You fellows seem to be afraid that you won't get enough to eat, when you carry such a good stock of provisions about with you;" and then our captain, after a few hurried words with the ship's captain, called out:

"Jump up on deck here, four of you. One will be quite enough in that boat to steer her;" and as I began to climb the ship's side, he stopped me, saying: "You can remain in the boat, my lad, and steer her. You've been steering her before, haven't you? And one of the other boats will take you in tow."

But Barney was not going to give up yet without making another effort, and said:

"We've got to go ashore, sir, anyway, to load up the boat."

"No," said Captain Ryan, "there is no necessity for your going; there are enough men and to spare," and looking at me, he said: "Tell Mr. Ringold when you get on shore to have the launch well loaded, and hurry up the work, and that I will be ashore again in the afternoon."

As soon as one of the other boats was ready, I was taken in tow in the launch, and on the way ashore, alone in the boat, I had time to think of and admire the tact displayed by Ryan in frustrating Barney's little plan, without leading him to suspect anything, and without compromising any one. The launch did make four trips with wood that day, and had to go ashore again at sundown to help the other boats to bring off the men. Then the oars were put in her, and Barney and his mates were allowed to pull her ashore; but there was no chance for desertion, as all the ship's boats were in the water and pulling ashore together. On the way ashore Barney talked and regretted bitterly the miscarriage of his plan, but he laid all the blame on himself.

"I might have known that," said he, "we couldn't go off to the ship so many times without the skipper or mates asking what we wanted the sails in the boat for. I'd have done it myself. What a cursed fool I was! We might have left them things in the encampment till the last trip, or stowed them away in the mangrove bushes until we wanted them. You fellows are just as bad. It's a wonder none of you thought of it. Yes, it's all up now, mates. We're booked for the war now sure enough, there's no getting out of it."

When we got back to the ship that night with the men, all the boats were hoisted on board and the ship got under weigh, although it was near midnight, and we steamed away to sea. At the first streak of daylight we steamed in for the land again, and early in the day we dropped anchor near Blewfields, a small town on the Mosquito Coast, a nigger or Sambo kingdom, set up by runaway slaves from the English West India islands. The inhabitants are principally Sambos, a cross between the Negro and the Indian. They have, or had at the time of our visit, a negro or Sambo king, and were not interfered with by the Nicaraguan Republic. We took some bullocks on board, and sailed the next day for Cuba. I was laid up sick with a low fever, and was never on deck until the Cuban coast was sighted.

One afternoon I heard the men talking on deck, and calling each other's attention to objects on shore, and wondering where the landing was to be made. Then I heard that it was decided to stand off the land that evening, and run in again in the night, and land our men at daylight, so it was about ship and out to sea again; and at night the ship's head was put about again for the land, and just before daylight we dropped anchor in a little wooded bay, and prepared to disembark men and arms. But we were not allowed to land so easily as we expected. I had dragged myself up from below, sick and weak in body, so much so as to be indifferent as to what became of me. I no longer cared for Cuba or the independence of her people. My backbone seemed to have gone out of me. I only wished to be let lie quietly anywhere. I heard the doctor say, "That youth is not fit to go on shore, he is too sick; he'll only be an incumbrance. Take him below and put him in his bunk, some of you," and two men offered to assist me below, but I begged of them to let me lie and rest awhile on deck, it was so hot and stifling down below, so they let me lie.

When daylight came we found that we were not the only vessel in the little bay; there was a Spanish war brig at anchor close in-shore on the further side, almost in the trees, and no doubt she was there in expectation and on the look-out for us, for I could hear from where I lay on the deck a drum beating on board of her, and she soon after fired a gun—I suppose as an intimation that she would like to know who we were, and what we wanted in that out-of-the-way place. There was a pile of wood on our deck between the after hatch and the main rigging, sloping up to the rail of the topgallant bulwark, and I crawled up this, on hearing the gun fire, in my curiosity to see what was going on, and lay stretched out on it, with my head resting on the rail. A boat was lowered and filled with men, and shoved off from the brig's side, pulling towards us; but our captain must have seen the brig before she fired the gun, for our chain-cable was unshackled abaft the windlass, and we slipped our anchor at the first roll of the drum, letting the chain run quietly out, and moved slowly away under steam.

In going in towards the land in the night we had furled all sail on board our vessel, and went in under steam, so that, luckily for us, we still had steam up, and were able to get out of the bay. When the brig saw that we took no notice of her, but were trying to get to sea, she recalled her boat and fired two shots at us; we paid no attention to her, but kept edging on to clear the east point of the bay. The brig now let fall all her canvas and slipped her anchor, for we could hear the chain rattling through her hawse-pipe as she let it go. She had a fair wind for us if she could only get out from under the lee of the trees and the land; but she was a sailing brig, and as we had steam power we had an advantage over her, if we could weather the point of land without being crippled by her shot.

As soon as her sails were sheeted home and mast-headed, she got all her boats out ahead to tow her into an offing, where she could feel the breeze and go for us; but if we could only weather the point safely, we could also make sail, and with wind and steam we could soon run out of range. All at once she seemed to catch the breeze, for her boats dropped alongside and were hoisted up to the davits, and then she opened fire on us with her bow guns, and her shot soon began to drop near and ahead of us; she was closing up on us fast, for we had to steam at right angles to her course to get round the point. Just before we cleared it I heard a crash and splintering of wood, so close as to startle me, and on sitting up I saw that a shot had come through the bulwarks and through the launch that was stowed amidships on deck, and passed out on the other side, severely wounding two of our men with splinters of wood. The men were requested to keep quiet and make as little noise as possible. Our sails were loosed and sheeted home, and as we rounded the point the topsails were mastheaded, and notwithstanding the injunction to keep quiet, three ringing cheers were given by the men in defiance and in answer to the fire from the brig. The men were getting very excited, and the captain of the ship shouted a volley of oaths at them for making such a noise, when a rush was immediately made for the 'tween decks, and in a few moments they were all on deck again, armed with their rifles.

and sabres, and shouting to the captain to put them alongside the brig. One big, piratical-looking fellow came aft with a crowd of men at his heels, all armed, and insolently asked the captain what he meant by swearing at them, and to take care how he spoke to them; that in speaking to them he was not speaking to his crew, and to remember that, as long as they were on board, they " bossed the hooker." And now, he said :

"We want you to bout ship and run alongside that dego brig, and we'll soon choke her luff."

While this was going on, I lay, or rather reclined on the wood heap, with my elbows resting on the rail, and looking over the side every now and again, watching the brig with all her canvas drawing, stunsails set alow and aloft, and a good curl of white water showing under her bow; whilst every now and again a puff of smoke would shoot out from her, as she sent shot after shot at us, to try and bring us to.

Our colonel spoke to the men and managed to quiet them and bring them to reason, telling them that even if we succeeded in taking the brig, it would only be after a severe loss, as we had no guns, and would suffer heavily from her battery without being able to reply, or do anything until we got alongside, yardarm to yardarm, and boarded her; and then in the event of her capture, it would be a useless victory for us, as we could make no use of her, we would have to burn her, and encumber ourselves with her crew as prisoners. That we would have to land them and let them go, when they could inform the Spanish authorities ashore of the landing of our expedition, our equipment, number of men, and place of disembarkation, all of which it was to our interest to keep secret. The majority of the men saw at once the necessity of this, but some of them said :

" Well, can't we get up the two guns that are in the hold, and have a crack at the Spaniard ? It's hard lines that he should have all the fun, and we be nothing but a target."

We had two nine-pounder field pieces on board, with their carriages, tumbrels, harness, and all appurtenances, intended for the expedition, and it was to these the men referred when they spoke about the two guns.

The colonel explained that they would be useless on board ship, as when mounted on their carriages they would stand too high to point through the ports in the bulwarks, and too low to point over the rail ; and that, in any case, there would not be room for the trails on the deck, as they were not ship's guns but field pieces, and altogether unsuitable for use on shipboard. But for that, he said, he would have had them up. I myself thought at the time that if

I was in charge or had any authority, I would get them up out of the hold, and manage to make use of them from our poop-deck, which was raised about four feet above the main-deck, or what would be called the spar-deck in a war vessel; and as we had now cleared the point, and were going off before the wind, with the brig astern of us instead of abeam, the guns would be *en barbette*, or raised above everything if they were placed on the poop, with plenty of room to work them, and they could be trained easily, within an arc of forty-five degrees, over the stern. I was of the same opinion as some of the men, and thought it hard to have to run away and receive all the pelting, without being able to make any return; but I was only a boy of seventeen then, and could not be expected to understand things as well as my commander. The men were satisfied with the colonel's explanation, and quietly dispersed.

While this was going on, the brig kept up her fire, and I was surprised that we were not struck oftener by her shot. I lay with my head on the rail looking astern at her, and watching every shot that she fired. Sometimes a shot would strike the water alongside of us, and sometimes away ahead. One shot struck a boat hanging in the davits over the starboard side where I lay, completely destroying it. I saw another strike the water astern, and ricochet high up and go through our foresail just under the foreyard. A foot higher up, and it would have crippled our foreyard; but such is the uncertainty of artillery at sea, firing from an irregularly moving vessel at another vessel in motion, that this was the only damage we suffered from the fire of the brig. When the men were all aft, crowded together in front of the poop, and talking to the officers, I expected every moment to see a shot go ploughing through them, leaving death and destruction in its wake, but I was agreeably surprised to find that we had escaped so well. We were going well through the water now, under both sail and steam, with the wind about two points on the starboard quarter, so as to fill all the sails, and I soon observed that the shot from the brig began to drop in the water astern; and she soon ceased firing altogether, as she was only wasting her ammunition, for we were out of range and fast leaving her. When our skipper saw that, he gave orders to set topmast stunsails, and stop steaming, and bank fires; and we kept on under sail only, the brig still keeping up the chase astern under a cloud of canvas.

I thought that when we got outside our skipper would steam to windward, where the brig could not follow us, as she was a sailing vessel, and thus we would get rid of her quickly; and I was surprised when I heard the order given to stop steaming and bank fires, for that left us at the mercy of the brig if we could not outsail her. But our skipper knew his ship and what she could do, for it was soon evident that under sail alone we could run away from the Spaniard, and by noon we had sunk her hull and courses. At five in the evening she was invisible from the deck, and could only be seen from aloft. Orders were then given to take in stunsails, clew up and furl sails, and every stitch of canvas on the ship was furled, and there we lay stripped in the open sea, like a log on the water, rolling from one side to the other; and as the vessel had no steerage way on her, and nothing to steady her, she was quite unmanageable, and fell into the trough of the sea, and although the weather was fine she rolled tremendously. Her lower yardarms would almost touch the water at times, but we had to put up with it until dark, when the fires were spread and steam got up again, and then away we went straight back for the land again under steam, passing the brig in the night, and of course leaving her dead to leeward, and making it impossible for her to interfere with us unless the wind changed.

The carpenters had been busy all day repairing the damages done to the boats by the fire from the brig. The launch was repaired in a rough sort of way, by nailing pieces of board over the shotholes, tarred canvas being first stretched over them;

but one of the boats that hung in the davits had to be broken up, as it was damaged beyond repair, and the men were set to work knocking the copper nails out of the woodwork of the boat and straightening them; anything to keep them employed.

CHAPTER VI.

We outmanœuvre the brig—Run in at night—Disembark men and arms—March for the interior—First encounter with the enemy—Sick men—Quartered at a sugar-mill—Pursuit of lighters on the river—Coopering—We decide to make a raft.

I FELT myself getting rapidly better, the excitement of the morning, the firing from the brig, and the threatened mutiny on board our own ship acting on me like a tonic; but I now learned that one of the two men who had been wounded in the morning had died; the other was my friend Barney, but he was not badly hurt. The man who died in the evening was buried at sea some time during the night, but the ship's way was not stopped, and there was no ceremony, such as we read of in cases of burial at sea; but the body was carried aft and a weight was tied to its feet, and it was launched over the taffrail.

I had been under fire for the first time in my life that day, and my sensations were—as well as I can recall them—utter indifference, although I was well aware—in fact, I exaggerated the danger—that at any moment a shot might go through me and end my career. I might have gone below at any time out of danger, comparatively, for I was sick and had no duty that required my presence on deck, and yet I sat there leaning over the side, devoid of fear, and never changed my position all the time we were under the brig's fire. I do not say this boastingly, but merely to show how sickness and suffering makes men indifferent to death.

The morning was far advanced before we drew in close to the land again, and as there was nothing suspicious in sight, a boat was lowered and sent ashore with two of our Cuban passengers, who were revolutionary agents; and after about two hours' delay, the boat came off without them, but it brought news that there was a Spanish war steamer on the coast looking for us, and as she might make her appearance at any moment, we were advised to defer making the landing until night. So we headed seaward again under sail, and at nightfall all sails were furled, topgallant yards and masts sent down, and the topmasts struck, and we steered once more for the land under steam. As we approached the land we seemed to go so close in that some of us thought the intention was to run the ship ashore and land the men at all hazard; but there was a

WE DISEMBARK. 69

Cuban on board who knew the coast well, and acted as our pilot, and brought us very cleverly and safely to an anchorage, and all hands were soon busy, hoisting out boats, getting up arms and ammunition out of the hold, and preparing to land. As soon as the boats were in the water and manned, we were told off, so many to each boat every trip. Besides our arms and ammunition, each man had two days' rations and a gray blanket served out to him; there were no knapsacks, but any man who had a spare shirt or other clothing, carried it rolled up in his blanket and slung over one shoulder.

Two days had made a wonderful improvement in me, and although I was weak, I felt well and in good spirits, and anxious to get on shore and begin the struggle. I was one of the first batch that landed, and the place we landed at was steep and thickly-wooded, and we were immediately extended in a line as sentries round and enclosing a space where the rest of the men and arms were to be landed. The landing was safely made and we were not disturbed, but it came on to rain during the night, and rained until daylight. As the day broke we looked out seaward to see if the ship was still there, for we did not know whether all the men and stores had been landed during the night; but there was nothing in sight but the sea and sky. The men had all been landed, and the ship had weighed anchor and was already out of sight, and we were left in Cuba to seek our fortunes, glory or the grave!

The two guns were not landed, as we heard that horses could not be procured easily in the neighbourhood, and the country thereabouts was difficult, and no roads practicable for artillery; so the guns remained on board, and also my quondam friend Barney, who was so badly hurt by a wood splinter that he was not landed. As soon as the sentries were relieved in the morning we had some coffee, and in the afternoon we moved about a mile inland, and encamped in a wood, where we were joined by a large body of patriots, as the Cubans were called.

We remained one day at this place, waiting for some mules, and at sundown we started on the march to join the main body of the Cubans, who were in the mountains in the interior of the island. We marched until midnight, when a halt was called, and we rested for a couple of hours; after which the march was resumed, and we trudged on without a stoppage until nine in the morning, when we encamped and prepared breakfast; and after eating it we lay down and slept until three or four in the afternoon, when we were roused up and had dinner, and started on the march again through wood and swamp until midnight; and as on the night before we were allowed a short rest, and marched

A SURPRISE.   71

again until the sun got unpleasantly hot about eight or nine, when we halted for breakfast and siesta. This was our almost invariable custom, as we avoided marching in the hot sun, and always encamped in a wood when possible, so that our numbers could not be well estimated by the enemy or his spies; for I believe it was given out that we were a large force, well provided with all necessaries, and with cavalry, infantry, and artillery, and had landed from several ships; and to keep up the deception we were kept under cover and as free from observation as possible. After a week's march through a difficult country, mostly swamp and bush, which left our clothes and foot-gear in a deplorable condition, we fell in with a party of the enemy, or rather they fell in with us. We were encamped, for our morning's siesta, under the shelter of some trees on the edge of an open savanna, where some of our Cubans had gone to cut grass, when they were surprised by a party of Spanish cavalry, and pursued back to the encampment. The enemy never drew rein when they came to the trees, as they were pretty open on the edge of the savanna, but dashed right into them in pursuit of the Cubans. We had scarcely time to seize our rifles and form up as they galloped past us, and we sent a volley into them that must have surprised them, for we were on their left flank, but they did not see us until they heard the report of our rifles; and the next moment, what was left of them were right on the Cubans, in among their camp fires; but the fight was over in a few minutes, for they were dragged from their horses and killed.

There were twenty-two men and an officer, and thirteen of them dropped from our fire, the other ten fell to the Cubans. Not a single one escaped ! From the time the alarm was first given until the last man was dead could not have been more than five minutes. The wounded who fell in front of us had their throats cut by the infuriated Cubans as they lay on the ground. This was short and sharp work, and did not speak well for the judgment of the Spanish officer, to charge into a wood on near six hundred men with his small party of twenty-two, but it gave us a foretaste of the war we were engaged in; a war of extermination, in which quarter was neither given nor expected on either side. Of the enemy's horses seven were either killed outright, or so badly wounded that they had to be killed, and we had a small ration of horse-flesh served out to us that afternoon; and as there were no more of the enemy supposed to be in our neighbourhood, we were allowed to rest, and did not march that afternoon, but feasted on horse-flesh, and mended, as best we could, our tattered clothing; we used up the uniforms of the dead Spanish soldiers for this purpose. I remarked that they were all young men of good physique, and some of them were as fair as Englishmen; their officer was a young fellow, and lay dead under a wounded horse; he had fallen at the first fire. All the men were dressed in cotton uniforms, of a narrow blue and white stripe, and wore white Panama hats; a very suitable uniform for a hot climate, and used at that time by the Spanish troops in Cuba. We dug a trench and laid them in it, covering them up with earth, and marked it with a rude cross made from the branches of the trees, and that was the end of them. In our subsequent encounters with the enemy we did not take this trouble with their dead, and contented ourselves with burying our own.

This first brush with the enemy was not much to boast of, certainly, but it seemed to put the Cubans in good spirits, and it had an exhilarating effect on our men also. We had come in contact with regular troops for the first time, and we had annihilated them. True, we were as twenty-five to one, and the result could not well have been otherwise; still, it was a victory, a success gained through the audacity and rashness of the Spanish officer, and although a small one, the *morale* of the men was improved by it. Three of the Cubans who were killed in the *mêlée* were interred with a little more ceremony. Each one was placed in a separate grave, and was honoured with a cross, on which his name was roughly cut; and at night a little hollow was scraped by the hand in the mounds of fresh earth, and lights were put in them by the friends of the dead men.

We broke camp at midnight, and marched on an *ingenio*, or sugar-mill and distillery, situated on the banks of a small river that we had to cross, and where we expected to find boats and lighters to pass us over. A good many of our men began to get sick with symptoms of diarrhœa and dysentery, brought on, no doubt, by our mode of living and food, which consisted of anything that we could procure on the march, principally plantains, bananas, and oranges, green and ripe, for we had no regular commissariat. We made slow progress on this march, although the ground was the best we had hitherto passed over. The company to which I belonged formed the rear-guard that morning, and we had to halt several times to allow the sick men to rest for a few minutes, or perform a necessary function of nature; and a general halt had to be made at daylight to allow all stragglers and the rear-guard to come up, for we had got spread out over two miles of ground, and the rear-guard had strict orders not to allow any one to remain behind. We were then only four leagues from the *ingenio*,

AT A SUGAR-MILL.

and a mounted party of Cubans were sent forward to reconnoitre. Comandante Fernandez, a Cuban officer, went with them, as he was anxious to surprise and capture the owner of the establishment, who was a native of old Spain, and a great friend of the Government. The sick and weak were mounted on all the available horses, mules, and carts, and after a short rest we followed, marching all day for the first time in the open under a tropical sun, with short stoppages to allow the people to keep well together, but never for longer than fifteen or twenty minutes. We arrived at the *ingenio* early in the evening to find the advanced party in possession, and to learn that the owner, on hearing of our approach, had embarked his family and loaded all his *caña*, or white rum, in his lighters and boats, and started down the river with all his principal workmen and *employés*. A few negroes and a mulatto *capataz*, or foreman, who remained in charge of the place, were instructed to tell us that the owner had left with the lighters two days previous to our arrival; but Fernandez doubted them, and had them tied up and flogged, until they confessed that they had only left a few minutes before the arrival of our party—a rather inquisitional and Spanish method of gaining information.

Fernandez had lost two hours in extorting this information, when leaving a guard at the *ingenio* to await our arrival, he started in pursuit of the boats and lighters with his best mounted men along the bank of the river; for not only the lighters and boats, but every stick of wood that would float, had either been taken away or destroyed at the mill, and it would be impossible for us to cross without them.

As the Cuban rivers are short and rapid, we might have marched up-stream and got round the head of the river in the event of not finding a suitable ford, but our leaders probably had reasons for not doing so, and an object in crossing at this place. It was, no doubt, the most direct route to where they wished to go. Besides, a rest was necessary for some of our men after the march through the swamps and woods from the coast. The *ingenio* was in a state of great confusion when we entered it; books and papers were scattered over the floors of the dwelling-house, and most of the furniture had disappeared. We could see that there had been ladies here, for articles of their dress and shoes that would fit no man's foot lay scattered on the floors, besides music-books and a piano. In the engine-house the boilers were still warm, and everything gave evidence that the place had only been evacuated a few hours before.

There were some cattle here feeding about in the open ground belonging to the establishment, and thirteen of them were caught and butchered for supper. We found also a small supply of yams, salt codfish, and jerked beef in the mill, and sugar and molasses seemed to have been thrown about everywhere.

It was lucky for us that we hit on this place, for I don't know what we should have done otherwise with our sick men. They were able to rest quietly here, and were properly attended to by our German surgeon and his assistant, who were then, as at all times, unwearied in their attendance on the sick and wounded.

The evening following our arrival at the *ingenio*, Fernandez and his party returned, with men and horses tired and hungry. He had, after hard riding, come up with the lighters and boats some miles down the river, and ordered them to pull in to the bank, and on their refusal he opened fire on them, which they returned. He followed them down the river, keeping up a running fight, but he could do very little damage to them, as they were well protected by the *caña* barrels and furniture that was piled up on the lighters; and as the banks of the river were low, and the lighters kept close to the opposite shore, he could make no impression on them, and got the worst of the fight in the beginning, for he had two men killed and four horses wounded, and that made him cautious; for he dismounted his men, and leaving the horses in charge of two men, he sought the shelter of the trees on the bank of the river and followed along, watching for every opportunity, when the enemy was off his guard or attempted to get his boats out ahead to tow the lighters, to have a shot at them. He obliged them to stop rowing and towing, and they had to keep the boats on the off-side of the lighters for shelter, and allow the lighters to drift down with the current. As night was coming on, without being able to do anything decisive, he determined to ride ahead in the hope of being able to find a bend, or narrow place, or high bank where he could act with effect, or perhaps fall in with a house down the river, where he could procure a boat or dug-out of some kind, and be enabled to cross over some of his men to the other side, and get the lighters between two fires as they came down the river. So he gave up the fight, mounted his men, and rode ahead down-stream until day began to dawn, when he turned his horses loose to allow them to feed for an hour.

He searched up and down the river bank to find a habitation, but all to no purpose. Neither could he find anything that he could make a raft out of, or any means of crossing; so choosing a favourable bend in the river where his men had good cover, and where the lighters would have to approach end

PURSUIT OF THE LIGHTERS.

on and be exposed to a raking fire, he lay down with his men to rest and wait for them. He had not long to wait; the lighters were soon seen coming down-stream in the middle of the river. Fernandez waited until they were about to turn to go round the bend, and then delivered his fire with good effect, for they became unmanageable for a few minutes, and one of them drifted so close to our side of the river, that for a moment Fernandez expected to be able to jump on board of her, if the enemy had not got a boat to pull her head round. As the boats were out ahead of the lighters now, and doing their best to tow them towards the opposite shore, Fernandez gave them another volley, and continued to fire on them, when a patrol of Spanish cavalry appeared on the opposite bank, attracted by the noise of the firing, and immediately took part in the skirmish.

The lighters hauled in to the opposite shore, and a consultation took place between the troopers and the lighter people. Fernandez knew that the lighters could not pass the enemy's cavalry over to his side without discharging their loading, and waited to see what they were going to do, and see if he could make out the force of the enemy and the result of the consultation. Of course the people in the lighters would know from Fernandez attacking them that we were probably at the *ingenio*, and would inform the troopers to that effect, although they did not know our numbers or the condition that we were in. Fernandez remained in the shelter of the trees on the river's bank until the lighters proceeded on their way down the river, the cavalry remaining all the time on the bank opposite; and after exchanging a few shots with them, as he could not find out their strength, he thought it better to get back and join us as quickly as possible. He was obliged to leave three of his horses behind him, they were so badly wounded as not to be able to travel, and he was wounded himself by a musket-shot in the left arm.

We were not idle in the meantime. Ridley, our commander, not knowing whether Fernandez would succeed in capturing the lighters, began to look about for some means of crossing to the other side of the river. All the barrels had been taken away, but in one shed we found a great many shooks, or bundles of staves, and heads, with bundles of hoop-iron, and kegs of rivets, and as there was a cooper's shop and tools in the place, as in all sugar-mills, all that we required was a few coopers to put them together. Any one who thought that he could put a cask together was allowed to try his hand, and after botching a few of them, we managed to muster three or four men who could cooper fairly well, and they were kept employed putting the casks together, with the object of building a raft to float ourselves, our arms, and ammunition across. Some of the men were engaged in pulling the roofs off the sheds to form a platform on the casks.

CHAPTER VII.

The *Ingenio*—A lesson in fortification—We intend to march on Bayamo — Comandante Fernandez — The Chigoe— Men dying—Party of enemy appear—We are sent in pursuit—Sufferings in a swamp—We find the enemy and lose two officers—Rumoured defeat of Cubans in the mountains.

THE dwelling-house, offices, and some other buildings in this place were at the foot of a little hillock, or ridge, that ran along on one side and parallel with the river, and on the top of this ridge were a row of trees growing, and joined together with a rough wooden fence. The ground sloped away from the fence towards the country, and to any one approaching the place from that side, only the chimney of the boiler-house and part of the roofs of the buildings would be visible between the trees. The walls were hidden and protected by the ridge of ground at the back of them, for the backs of the buildings faced the country, the fronts looking towards the river, or the enclosed space of the mill yard. Our commander took advantage of the ground, and laid out a ditch some twenty yards outside the fence on the sloping ground, and the men were put to work on it. The earth was thrown to the front of the ditch, and inside the fence a step was cut in the bank, and the earth thrown on top on the outside, so that the step formed the banquette for the men to stand on, and the earth thrown up on the ridge helped to form the parapet, and protected the men firing from behind it. Some men were sent to fell trees a little way along the bank of the river, both above and below the mill on our flanks, as there was no protecting ridge there. The ditches were made between the trees, and the trees were left standing to a short distance in front of the outer ditch, but beyond that they were cut down, with the double object of clearing a space in front, so as not to afford cover to the enemy in case we should be attacked here, and of trying to form a raft with them, in case that our amateur coopers should fail in making watertight casks; perhaps, also, with the object of keeping the men employed, for there were not spades and shovels sufficient, and some of the men working at the ditches had to throw the earth out with their hands. This work was pretty well advanced when Fernandez got back, and the next day finished it, with the addition of zig-zag ditches, that led from the outer ditch to the inside of the fence.

We were in fairly comfortable quarters for the first time since we landed, with a good supply of food, and where our sick men could rest and recruit themselves, with no force of the enemy in our neighbourhood strong enough to attack us, and we felt secure in our position. While the materials for the raft were being prepared, our Cuban friends had time to look around, pick up recruits, and gain information. Two *baqueanos*, or scouts, who knew the country, were sent to inform the main body of the Cubans of our landing and progress, and two more were sent back to the coast, with the same information to our friends there, and with instructions for the guidance of any other force that should happen to land; for we were still a long distance from the main body of the insurgents, and would have to make a detour to reach them, as there were Spanish forces of importance between us and them, and unless we received large additions to our little force, we could not venture to attack them with any hope of success. It was the intention of our leaders, as soon as we crossed the river, to swerve to the right, and march directly on the city of Bayamo, and carry it by assault, when they expected the whole surrounding district would rise against the Spaniards, and we would be then strong enough to operate against Santiago de Cuba, where a large Spanish force was quartered, and perhaps our Cuban friends in the mountains would be able to join us instead of our joining them.

As soon as the horses had a day's rest, two parties of Cubans were sent to scour the country around the mill and collect cattle and horses, and as many of their compatriots as possible, to swell our commissariat and our ranks. Fernandez did not go with them, as his wound was exceedingly painful. I rather liked Fernandez. He was a tall, good-looking fellow about thirty-five, and had taken part in several risings in the island, so that it was nothing new to him. He spoke English fairly well, as did several of the Cuban officers who were with us, but he appeared to me, like most of his countrymen, to have had a lick of the tar-brush. But he was a brave man, a good soldier, and a favourite with our men.

Here at this sugar-mill I made my first acquaintanceship with the "chigoe," or the "jigger," as the men called it, a little insect very common in the West Indies. We used to go about bare-footed, as many of us had no shoes, and those who had wished to save them for the march. When we had been about two days here, I felt a great itching in the big toe of my right foot, in close by the nail, and after rubbing it hard, I remarked to one of the men, a sailor named Jackson, that there was something coming on my toe, and it was so itchy I did not know what to do, as I had to be continually scratching it.

"Let me see it," said Jackson. "Why, that's a jigger. You must get that out without delay and without breaking it, or it will spread all over your leg. I'll get a needle and take it out for you."

Jackson got a fine sewing needle, and taking my foot up on his knee, began with the point of the needle to pick the skin away from around the itchy place, until he exposed a little bladder-like sac, about a sixteenth of an inch in diameter. He worked under this with his needle until he got it clean out, and all was done without drawing a drop of blood; then taking some tobacco ashes from his pipe, he filled the little hollow in my toe with it, and taking a leaf of the same weed from a plug that he carried in his pocket, and wetting it in his mouth, he wrapped it round the toe, and tying a piece of rag over all, told me that it was all right.

When we broke the little sac we found it full of little white nits, or seeds, and Jackson told me that in taking them out one should be careful to avoid breaking the sac, for if one of the small seeds remained in the flesh, it would grow and spread all over the foot and leg; and he had seen negroes with legs like elephants', caused by the jiggers getting into them and not being removed in time. I wore shoes every day after this while they lasted, but it was a common occurrence for the men to have to take jiggers out every day while we remained here. Even the men who wore boots and shoes were troubled with them. The insect itself is so small as scarcely to be seen by the unaided eye.

While we remained here we were drilled every morning and evening, and although we could not complain on the score of food, our sick list was getting alarmingly large. There were about forty men laid up with dysentery; six died on the fifth or sixth day after our arrival. On the same day a small party of the enemy appeared on the opposite bank of the river, but disappeared when we fired on them. From the roofs of the buildings and the tops of the trees we made them out to be ten mounted men, probably the same party that Fernandez met down the river when he went in pursuit of the lighters. We felt greatly the want of a small boat or some means of crossing the river, and it was decided to rig up a catamaran out of some of the barrels that were already put together, so that a party could cross and throw up some defensive work, or place obstacles in the way, that would prevent the enemy from coming up to the bank directly opposite the mill; for the mill, and everything about it, could be examined from the opposite bank. A catamaran was made out of nine casks, and floored. And as the foraging and recruiting parties arrived back that evening, bringing in a few cattle and horses with them, it was resolved to pass over some men and horses with the aid of the catamaran that night, and send them in pursuit of the enemy, as it was feared that they had noted our force and position, and would soon carry or send that information to their head-quarters.

I may here say that all our men were armed with "Minié" rifles and bayonets, with the exception of the artillery company to which I belonged; we had swords instead of bayonets, and carried the "Minié" rifle the same as the infantry. I also had a revolver, my own property, a muzzle-loader — breech-loaders were not then introduced. Twenty-eight men were picked out of the artillery company, and horses were given to us, and we were ordered to be ready for crossing the river at dark. In four or five trips of the catamaran we passed everything over, swimming the horses across, and we slept on the bank until daybreak, when the order was given to saddle up. We had a few Cubans and a Cuban officer in our party, who were supposed to know the country, and we rode along the left bank of the river up-stream. We scoured the country in that direction all day without falling in with any of the enemy, and at nightfall we rode up to a house where we intended to pass the night. Here we were told that no Government troops had been seen in that neighbourhood. At daylight we were in the saddle again, riding east, and making inquiries at every place we passed, but no enemy was seen. We unsaddled for a few hours in the middle of the day to rest and feed our horses, and again started on the march. In the evening we were riding through swampy ground, with the water over the fetlocks of our horses, and sometimes up to their knees. The night closed in on us, and we were still jogging along through this swamp. The Cubans in our party told us that we would soon be clear of the water, and get on higher ground; but we plodded wearily along until at last our horses got tired and refused to move further, leaving us there in the swamp. It was then past midnight, and there was no remedy for it but to dismount and wait for daylight. The water reached half-way to our knees, and the swamp grass and weeds in some places were away above a man's head on horseback. The mosquitoes were terrible; and I rarely passed a more miserable night anywhere. We tried to move on on foot, leading our horses after us by the bridle; but after a few yards they stuck and refused to move, so we loosed the girths and took the bits out of their mouths, so that they could pick a mouthful of the swamp grass, while we drew our swords and cut down the long grass and reeds around us. We opened up a good wide circle with our sabres, and by collecting all the long grass and weeds together in a heap, we were enabled to raise ourselves out of the water, and lie down on it; but it was no use trying to sleep, the mosquitoes were too many for us. Every now and again some one, maddened by the mosquitoes and other insects, would start up and rush down off the heap into the swamp, kicking the water, and uttering maledictions on the place, the country, and the people, the expedition, and the day that they joined it, the ship that brought them, and everything connected with it.

Many soldiers and sailors are so accustomed to swearing and interlarding their conversation with oaths and imprecations, often meaningless, that many of them seem not to be able to express themselves without an oath or profanity. It was the only way they could give vent to their feelings and ease their tempers that night, and it did seem to relieve them, for after a deep oath, or string of imprecations, a man would cool down for a while and remain quiet, probably shocked at, or ashamed of his own profanity, until the mosquitoes had again worked his temper up to the exploding point, when he would break out again with a new malediction.

Morning came at last, and we were not long in saddling up and mounting, and after an hour's march we got out of the swamp, and jogged on our tired horses towards an orange grove that we saw on some high ground, surmising that a house could not be far away; and we were right in our surmise, for we found a house in the orange grove, and we decided to unsaddle and rest ourselves and our horses until the afternoon, for neither men nor horses were in a fit state to meet the enemy. The owner of the house was a friend to the insurgent cause, but he had bad news for us. He told us that it was rumoured that the insurgents had been defeated and dispersed by the Government troops in the interior. He could not say whether there was any truth in the rumour, or whether it was a report spread by the Government partisans, to discourage the people from joining the insurgents. He had not seen any troops; and after hearing from us where we had been the two days previous, he informed us as to the direction probably taken by the enemy.

We saddled up early in the afternoon, and marched in the direction pointed out to us by our guide, and soon found ourselves in another swamp, but of inconsiderable extent, for we were soon across it and on good ground, and rode on, only stopping for about twenty minutes before sundown to have a supper of bananas, and fill our haversacks, as we passed through a grove of very fine ones. As the sun was setting, we noticed a house on a rising ground before us, and a halt was immediately called, until Ringold, our lieutenant, and the Cuban officer, had examined it through their field-glasses. After a long look they told us that the enemy's party that we were in search of were found at last, and we prepared to meet them.

We dismounted and looked to our arms, and held our horses by the bridles until it got darker, when we tightened up our girths and advanced towards the house on foot, leading our horses by the bridle. Our orders were to capture or destroy the whole party at any sacrifice, and by approaching the house on foot, we could see better any movement made by the enemy round and about it, and be better able to take him by surprise. We had to walk down a gently sloping ground, cross a little swampy brook, and ascend a gradually rising ground to the house. When we were about a hundred yards off we halted, and both our officers went forward to reconnoitre. After some delay they rejoined us, the horses were left in charge of two men, and we again advanced, creeping up to within forty or fifty yards of the house, and surrounding it. Ringold and the Cuban officer mounted their horses and rode boldly up to the house, and called on the Spaniards to surrender, telling them that they were surrounded by superior forces, and that it would be useless for them to resist. The Spaniards answered by shooting Ringold and the Cuban dead, and then rushed for their horses. As there were some fires burning in the *patio*, or space in front of the house, where the enemy was cooking his supper when we came upon him, we could see what was taking place near the house, and on seeing both our officers shot down, we fired a volley at the enemy and closed in on him. Josiah Storey, a Boston lad, who was at the back of the house, had crept up quite close, and when he heard the firing in front, he thrust the muzzle of his rifle into the thatch of the roof and fired it off, and in a moment the house was in a blaze. In the scrimmage which followed we made four prisoners, two of them wounded, and the other six got clear away. It would have been useless for us to follow them in the night, as we did not know the country, and they might lead us into the hands of a stronger party; but in any case, the condition of our horses made it impossible for us to follow them, for they were scarcely able to move in a slow trot, and as both our officers were dead, it behoved us to get back to the mill as soon as possible.

In half an hour the rancho, or house, was reduced to ashes, and the owner, a mulatto, and his wife were secured with the other prisoners. We built a big fire in the space in front of the ruins of the house, and sat round it and talked all night, for although we were fatigued with our day's ride on tired horses — and nothing fatigues a man more than urging on a tired horse—we could not sleep. Unfortunately, one of the men found a demijohn of *caña,* or white rum, that escaped the fire somehow, and they were beginning to make themselves happy with it, as there was no one to control them but Smith, a sergeant, and he was as fond of liquor as any of them. Young as I was, I knew the danger and the risk we ran if the men were allowed to get drunk there, and as I had no authority to prevent them from drinking, I determined to stop their grog in another way. I watched for an opportunity when no one was looking at me, and quietly took the stopper out of the demijohn, and tilted it up on its side, with the neck inclined down, and I placed the stopper under it to prop it in that position, so when the next man went to replenish his tin panakin, he found the demijohn capsized and empty. Then there was a great outcry, and inquiry as to who was the awkward fellow that spilt all the good liquor. One fellow accused me, and said that he saw me last at it, but I protested that I never tasted rum in my life, and that I was not going to begin there. One fellow unwittingly took my part by saying:

"Oh, he didn't capsize it. I know he doesn't

take grog, and what would he be doing near it? Some of you fellows that were in too great a hurry did it, and now we have to sit here all night without a drop. Is there none at all left? Let's see." And taking the demijohn, he turned it up, and managed to drain about half a gill out of it, and saying, "I think I'm entitled to this," he drank it off, and that was the last of the rum.

We passed the night in talking round the fire, and the men expressed themselves freely as to our prospects, and commented on our chances of success or failure. Taking into account the news that we had heard the day before, and seeing small parties of Government troops scouring the country, it looked as if there was some truth in the rumour that the insurgents were defeated and dispersed, and that those small mounted parties were hunting them down. If it were not the case, we could not imagine why the Spanish commanders should split up their commands into the small parties that we were continually meeting on our march.

Some of the men took a gloomy view of our situation, and predicted disaster. They said that they believed that there was no Creole army, and that we, and the few Cubans who were with us, were the only forces opposed to the Government troops, and that on the slightest reverse the Cubans would desert us and go to their homes, and leave us to the mercies of the Spanish forces. As things turned out afterwards, there was a good deal of truth in these surmises of the men. Some of them did not think that things were so bad, and if they thought so, they would seize the raft as soon as they got back to the mill, and float down to the mouth of the river, and trust to chance to be able to capture some small vessel to get away in.

CHAPTER VIII.

Burial of our officers—Our first prisoners—Return to the *Ingenio*—Arrive in time to take part in the fight.

AT break of day we buried poor Ringold and the Cuban officer on the spot where they fell. On Ringold was found a trifle of money, a woman's likeness, and a few letters, that were taken in charge by Smith, the sergeant, to be delivered to Colonel Ridley on our return to head-quarters; one of the Cubans who was with us searched his dead countryman, and took charge of whatever effects he had on him. As soon as the graves were filled in, we ate our breakfast of bananas and saddled up our horses, and then debated as to what to do with the prisoners. A good many of the men wished to shoot them on the spot, but some of us were in favour of taking them with us to the mill, to let the commander decide how they were to be treated. It took a good deal of argument to persuade the men to adopt this view. The majority wanted them shot on the spot, and the few Cubans who were with us were surprised that there should be any hesitation in putting an end to them, and if they were allowed, or if they had not been in such a small minority in our party, they would soon settle the matter by cutting their throats. One man proposed to shoot the two wounded men, as there were not horses for all, and if we took them with us, two would have to ride double, and he was not going to let any *dego* ride with him.

"They'll die, anyhow," said he, "and let us put them out of pain."

The sergeant demurred to this, and said that he would not take the responsibility of it.

"Who wants you?" said Williams, a New Yorker. "I'll take the hull responsibility, if you're afraid. You're a fine sergeant, if you can't shoot four *degos* without talking of your responsibility!"

Smith, the sergeant, was an ex-navy officer, and had been made a sergeant on the voyage out, owing to his knowledge of drill and discipline; but the men treated him with scant respect. He had the education of a gentleman, but would get drunk whenever he had the opportunity, and probably he lost his position in the navy through drink. When sober he was right enough, and I have seen him behave well and distinguish himself, on more than one occasion.

Peterson, a Norwegian who was one of our party, said:

"Look, poys, I tink dat it is petter to take dis jung poy's advice, an' not shoot dose Spanish fellows, pecause if de news is true dat de insurgents is peten up to de mountains, ve vil have very ruff times in dis country, I tell you; an' if dose Spanish fellows katch us, dey vil cut all our troats, so I say 'tis de bes' ting to treat you prisoners vel, cos you don't know ven you mite pe a pris'ner yo'self, dat's my opinion."

"Well, you have no chance of escaping, anyhow, Peterson, if you fall into their hands," said Williams, "for they'd cut your throat for ugliness, if for nothing else."

Seeing that they were beginning to joke over it, I thought it good time to intercede for the prisoners, when little Storey almost spoiled it by turning to one of the Cubans, and saying, "Well, Antone, *savey*, cut the throat?" at the same time making a motion with his hand across his own throat, and pointing towards the Spaniards. "Bueno, or no bueno, eh?"

The Cuban understood the sign, if he did not understand the language that Storey intended for Spanish, for he answered:

"*Si, si, mejor degollarlos de una vez*"—"yes, yes, better cut their throats at once." However, they finally agreed to take the prisoners to head-quarters, but with the condition that, if they gave the least trouble on the march, or if we fell in with the enemy before reaching the mill, they were to be shot.

We started on the march back with the prisoners securely fastened, but had scarcely gone a mile, when a Cuban, who was leading as guide, pulled up and dismounted, and the rest of us rode forward to see what was the matter, for cavalry on the march ride in single file. We saw a Spanish soldier lying dead in the grass. He lay there with a stream of blood from his mouth, and must have been shot through the lungs, and yet he had been able to mount his horse and get away, and ride at full gallop a mile before he fell dead; it would almost seem impossible, yet there he was, one of the men who escaped from the house the night before, for he was recognised by the prisoners as one of their party.

As we started forward again it began to rain, and rained all day at intervals, and at night we put up at a deserted house, and had to be contented with a few green cobs of maize for supper. We found the house swarming with ants, so we did not venture inside, but camped in the *patio*, or yard; and as everything was soaking wet, we could not light a fire without firing a shot; that we did not care to do, and although we had no sleep the night before, we found it impossible to get any here. I pitied the prisoners, for their hands being tied they could not use them to keep the mosquitoes away from their faces; and three of us —Driscol, Ashton, and I—proposed to untie them, but the others would not hear of it; we offered to stand sentry over them all night, and be responsible for them, but all to no purpose, so we sat and fanned them and ourselves until morning.

At daylight we were again in the saddle and on the march, and expected to reach the mill before night; and in all that day's ride we found nothing edible on the ground we rode over, and many of us dozed in the saddle as we jogged along. I must have slept soundly for over an hour, for my horse stumbling woke me up. I thought I was falling from a height, and clutched at the horse's mane to save myself from tumbling off his back. About three in the afternoon we struck the bank of the river, and began to coast it up, as we knew that we were below the mill, and half an hour later we heard firing up the river, and hurried forward, as we supposed there was fighting going on at headquarters. As we drew near the firing grew heavier, until at last we came in sight of the open place on the opposite bank, where our fellows had cut the trees down. We moved back a little from the river's bank, so as not to be seen by the enemy, if he was on the other side, and hurried on our march; and when we judged that we were fairly abreast of the opening, we dismounted, and leaving our horses, unslung our rifles and advanced on foot to the river's bank, at the same time making our prisoners advance with us. We were in time to see some of the enemy's men cross the open space between the trees to attack the mill. Our men were receiving them hotly, and we came close up to the bank of the river unperceived, and delivered our fire on their flank. It was so unexpected that they hesitated for a moment and looked across the river at us, and seemed undecided whether to advance or retreat, until their leader spoke to them and cheered them on, and they gallantly rushed forward again to the attack. But the attack failed, and in a few minutes they were again crossing the open, and exposed to our fire; and as they disappeared in the trees, some of our men from the mill appeared in pursuit of them, led by Ryan, the captain of my company, who shouted to us to go down along the bank of the river and watch for them. We did so, but without being able to see anything more of them, as they did not retreat by the river, and we returned in the evening completely fagged out.

On arriving in front of the mill and reporting

ourselves, we got orders to turn our horses loose, as they were too tired to stray far, and cross over ourselves, and a ponton, or raft, was sent across for us; and after giving an account of our proceedings, the fight with the Spaniards, and the loss of the two officers, our prisoners were turned over to Fernandez, and we went to get something to eat and a much-needed rest. I afterwards heard that the prisoners were shot that same night after being examined, by order of Fernandez.

CHAPTER IX.

Changes—Ridley sick—Messengers from the junta request us to hurry forward—We evacuate the mill—On the march—Mule-driving—Storey's plan—Dead men—Captains Ryan and Wingate.

THERE had been a great many changes at the mill in our absence. Many of the men had died, and there were many sick; some of the greatest blackguards in our force were dead or sick. As my friend Ashton said: "Wouldn't it be a blessing if all the blackguards were to die at once, or get killed right off?" But I am afraid our force would have been very much reduced in that case. Colonel Ridley was laid up sick, and we did not recognise some of the men, they looked so ill.

A messenger had arrived from the revolutionary junta with a request that our force would join them at once in the mountains; and from the scraps of information that we picked up, it appeared that the insurgents were in a bad way, if not already defeated and dispersed. We had to assist in burying the dead before we were allowed to sleep; not men killed in action, but men who died in the sheds, that day and the night before, from dysentery. Our men pursued the enemy only a short distance, and soon returned again to the mill. We slept soundly that night in spite of the moans of some wounded men who were near us, and the sun shining on my face woke me up in the morning; and one of the first things that I remarked was, the Cubans who were with our force did not muster as numerously as when we started on our scouting expedition five days ago; they had no doubt received information through their friends, which was withheld from us, of some disaster, or the collapse of the insurgent cause. Our party had been given up as captured and shot by the enemy, when we did not return on the third day, and it was an agreeable surprise to the officers to find us appearing at a very opportune moment on the bank of the river, and on the enemy's flank, when he thought it was secured by the river.

After having some coffee in the morning, a party was detailed to bury the dead, and another mounted party were sent to reconnoitre and see if the enemy had retired, or if they were still hanging about, and the remainder of the force were employed in getting everything ready to cross the river. In a few hours the reconnoitring party returned, and reported no enemy in sight anywhere, and we prepared at once to cross the river. All the sick men were sent over, and all the stores and ammunition, and lastly, the mules and horses. It was late when we got through with this operation, and the rafts were hauled out of the water and broken up. No delay was made on the bank of the river, and we began our march immediately for the mountains. The horses and mules were given up to the sick and wounded, with the exception of what were wanted for the transport of ammunition and stores; the sick and wounded rode also on the ammunition carts.

I now had my first experience in mule-driving. When we landed on the coast, those of our force who knew anything about horses, or could ride well, were selected for the artillery company, although our guns had been left on board; still, there was the hope that we might be able to supply ourselves from the enemy. There were a good many Cubans in the company who had their own horses, and while they rode, we marched on foot. The Cubans also drove the mule carts, as they understood the management of them better than we did, and whenever we were sent on any service that required mounted men, we were horsed by the Cubans. As many of them had disappeared while the expedition was at the mill, taking their horses with them, we found ourselves short of mule-drivers, and our company had to supply them; so I found myself in charge of a pair of mules, attached to a little country cart loaded with ammunition. I had read and heard a good deal about the mule, what a patient, hardy, and useful animal it is, and how it would be impossible to get along in some parts of the world without him. He may be so, for we found him useful in one respect, when we lived on his flesh at San Jacinto; but the pair I drove were as lazy and stubborn—well, as mules. I have never seen more worthless animals; they were in good condition, fat and well fed, and their load was not heavy, for four men could pull the little cart and its load with ease along the road; yet it was one continual flog, flog, unceasingly, to get them to move at a slow walk. My arms ached with flogging, and I seemed to suffer more than the mules. The men often had to assist, and shove cart and mules along together before them. In front of me was Storey, while behind me came Ashton, driving a similar team of mules. I used to belabour mine for near an hour at a time—in fact, until I was tired. When I stopped the mules stopped, and I had to sit down for a few minutes' rest, and take off my grey flannel shirt, and wring the perspiration out of it, and put it on again; then after wiping my face with my soft felt hat,

I was ready to go on again, and with a muttered curse on all the mules that were ever foaled, I began the flogging again. But my curses were not always silent ones, they were only so while I was new to the work. At first I felt ashamed of myself and of any one near hearing me; but that soon wore off, and with every mile travelled over, as my temper got ruffled, my profanity increased, until in the end I could scarcely believe my own ears, and could swear as hard as any old salt.

Storey, with Yankee ingenuity, tried several dodges to keep his mules moving. He collected some dry reeds and trailing plants on the road, and formed them into a flambeau, and he thought it would be much easier on himself to apply the lighted torch to the mules' hind-quarters when they refused to move, than flogging them with a whip. When he tried it, he said:

"Jerusalem! you should see them go; the brutes actually ran fifty yards without stopping! I was going back to tell you to try it, but I thought I'd go and start the mokes on a few yards further first; but it was no go, the brutes kicked at me when I came near them, and I had to give it up."

He next got two mess tins out of the cart he was driving, and tied them to the mules' tails, thinking to frighten them on; but they refused to move at all, until they were taken off. I have since learned that *machos*, or male mules, are not as good as *hembras*, or females, and always fetch a lower price. Ours may have been males, and if so, that would account for their worthlessness.

Our march led through open country for the first few miles; but by nightfall we were travelling through wooded country. We halted at midnight in a banana and plantain grove for supper and a short rest, and after loading ourselves with as many bananas and plantains as we could carry, we resumed our march until daylight, when another halt was called for an hour's rest and coffee. As we were preparing to start on the march again after coffee, two of the sick men were found dead in the carts, and were lifted out and left with the rearguard to be buried. I caught sight of Colonel Ridley while we were having coffee. He was reclining on a mat on top of some ammunition boxes in one of the little carts, and looked very sick, so much so that I barely recognised him; Captains Ryan and Wingate, with the German doctor, were standing round him, talking to him. Ryan had his arm under his head and shoulders supporting him while the doctor was trying to get him to take something he had in his hand. From the glimpse I got of him, I inferred that he could not last much longer, and for him it mattered little how the expedition ended. How different he appeared now to what he did a few short months ago, when he addressed us on the deck of the *Darthula* !

I will here try and describe Ryan and Wingate, both brave men and good soldiers, but of very different temperaments, as they were the last surviving officers of the expedition. Wingate, for all I know, may be living still, for I have not seen his name among those who were shot or garroted in Havana months after I had made my escape from Cuba; an account of which I read in an English newspaper. Ryan was the captain of my company, and the one I knew best. He fell riding in front of me, and died a soldier's death, sword in hand—at least, I hope so—I hope that he died there and then, and did not fall alive into the hands of the enemy, for he was too brave and gallant a soul to be executed like a criminal. But I am anticipating.

Captain Ryan was an American of Irish parentage, and like Colonel Ridley, had served in the Mexican War. He was a man of about five feet ten in height, square-built, straight as a lath, and thin, very thin; wiry, lithe, and agile as a cat; his hair was dark-brown, turning to gray, his features were regular and clean-cut, and he was one of those men who grow very little beard, although I may have been mistaken, for he was always clean-shaven like a priest; he had large, dark-gray eyes, with a melancholy, far-away look in them when at rest, but they fairly blazed in his head when he was excited; yet I have rarely seen a man who could command his temper as he could. I could not tell his age, he might have been any age from thirty to fifty. He never lost his head under any provocation or difficulty. When everything went well he "didn't show much," as the men said, but when difficulties and disaster overtook us, he was the one man to look to; he rose to every emergency. No danger appalled him, he was never wanting in an expedient to avert or mitigate an evil; he was a born soldier and leader of men, a man who inspired confidence in all those under him. Any project or enterprise, no matter how difficult or impossible it appeared of accomplishment, when he proposed it one felt instinctively that it was feasible, and he never hesitated to lead himself. He was the bravest man I ever knew, with nothing of the swash-buckler about him. One had only to look in his face to see that he was kindly and good-natured. A woman, perhaps, would not think him good-looking, or be likely to fall in love with him at first sight; but he was just the kind of man that men love and glory in. Poor Ryan! He was worthy of a better fate than to die in a miserable skirmish on the banks of a lonely Cuban river!

Wingate was a New Englander, between twenty-five and thirty years of age, and over six feet in height, a blue-eyed, fair-haired, powerfully built fellow, and the strongest man in the expedition. I recollect the night we landed on the coast, I somehow got into the wrong boat, when Wingate, to save delay, caught hold of me by the belt, and lifted me out of my seat, with my rifle, sword, ammunition, blanket, and three days' provisions attached, and passed me over his head and those of the other men, to the surprise of everybody, and dropped me into my proper place in the other boat, as if I had been a mere child. He seemed to have had some military training, but was a man of ungovernable temper, something of a bully, and always took the worst view of things. There was nothing of the cool, calculating Yankee about him; but he was a good soldier, and a splendid fellow in a fight, and I owed my life to him on one occasion. I hope that he made good his escape on that never-to-be-forgotten night, the last time I saw him, when the enemy and misfortune overtook us, and we were defeated and dispersed.

CHAPTER X.

Marching through forest—Shooting a Spanish scout—Attack on our rear—Enemy following us—Our chiefs decide to wait for them—Ride ahead and select our ground—Prepare for battle.

As we advanced on our march the wood on both sides of the road became more open, and about midday coming to a suitable place, we wheeled off the road and went into camp for rest and refreshment. After unhitching and attending to the mules, we had our usual breakfast of plantains and bananas, and tired out with my exertions in getting my mules along, I threw myself on the ground, with my face down and my head pillowed on my arms, and in a few minutes was fast asleep.

I must have been asleep a couple of hours, when I was awakened by the barking of a little dog that had followed us from the sugar-mill, and attached himself to Ashton; and sitting up, I found the men about me threatening and calling on the dog to be quiet and lie down. Ashton started to his feet, and saying that there must be something to make the dog bark in that way, walked over to and across the road, the dog running on before him and barking persistently. I got on my feet also, and caught sight of the Panama hat of a mounted Spanish soldier amongst the trees on the opposite side of the road. Although startled by what I saw, I did not lose my presence of mind, or alarm the men by shouting that the enemy was upon us, for I thought that only a small body of mounted men could have come up with us, or that it was one of the mounted patrols that we had often fallen in with before. I seized my rifle, and without uttering a word, rushed after Ashton.

From where the Spaniard sat on his horse among the trees on the rising ground, he could overlook our camp, partly, through an opening in the foliage, and he was evidently taking note of us, and trying to find out our equipment. I ran across the road, and entered the trees on the other side in time to see Ashton seize the Spaniard's bridle-rein, and call to him in English, saying: "Come, old boy, tumble off your nag and come along with me." The Spaniard drew a pistol, put it to Ashton's face, and fired. He dropped the reins and staggered back, and the Spaniard, from whom I never took my eyes, wheeled his horse and made off through the trees, where I lost sight of him.

The wood was not open enough for him to gallop, or move very fast through it, and from the shaking of the branches, I could see that he was going towards the road in a diagonal direction, so that, when he got there, he could make good his retreat at full gallop down the road. I immediately ran back to the road and dropped on my right knee, and using my left leg to rest the elbow of my left arm on, and steady my rifle, I cocked and levelled it, and with palpitating heart awaited him. Out he came on the road, almost as soon as I had taken up my position. He came out much further down than I expected, and I was trembling with excitement and fear that I should miss him, and leave my comrade's death unavenged; but with an effort I forced myself to keep cool, for I knew that everything depended on it, and allowing the foe to straighten himself on the road, I aimed between his shoulders and fired.

A feeling of intense satisfaction, almost delight, shot through me, as I saw him double in the saddle, and the next moment roll off his horse, the horse continuing his way riderless at full gallop down the road. Without waiting to reload, I ran down the road to where the Spaniard lay, and found him dead. Some of the men were on the ground almost as soon as I was, and one of the first was Ashton, who I thought lay shot through the head up in the bush; but he escaped almost by a miracle. His face was so close to the Spaniard's pistol when he fired that his hair and eyebrows were singed, and one side of his face was scorched and blackened. We searched the body, and found three dollars in money, a bundle of cigars, and a pocket-book on it. The dead man, it appeared, had been a sergeant, from the chevrons on his arm, and was dressed in the uniform of the Spanish soldier in Cuba—blue-and-white striped jacket and trousers, and broad-leafed Panama grass hat.

Ashton and I divided the three dollars and the cigars, and gave the pocket-book to the captain of our company. In less than a minute the slain man was stripped of everything on him; one man appropriating his jacket, another his hat, another his boots, and so on, for our men were rather short of clothing, and the uniforms of the Spanish soldiers were very useful when we could get them, for wrapping round our feet and legs, to protect them in our march through the woods and swamps.

We resumed our march in the midst of a heavy shower of rain, but a short distance from the encampment the ground began to slope in the direction we were travelling, and made the draught easier on the mules, although they still required a good deal of flogging to get them to move along.

After about two hours' rain, the weather cleared up,

and later on we heard firing in our rear; as we were not halted, and the firing soon ceased, we could not tell the cause of it, and could only conjecture that there was, as Storey said, "some rumpus astern." We toiled along the muddy road until dark, the undergrowth on each side being so thick and close that we could not leave it to encamp, and we bivouacked where we halted, right on the roadway.

With the night came the rain again, and we huddled under the little carts for what shelter they could afford us. Sitting on our hams, we ate our supper of bananas; towards morning the weather cleared, and we managed to light a fire and make coffee, after which we sat smoking and chatting, awaiting the order to hitch up and march; but no order came, and we were beginning to think that something serious had happened, when our captain came down the road with the rest of the company all mounted, and carrying spades and axes besides their arms; some Cubans and an officer came with them, and the mules and carts were turned over to them, for which we were not at all sorry, and we mounted their horses, and taking their tools, rode ahead with the rest of the company. We now learned the cause of the firing the evening before.

The enemy were following us up with a strong force. Their advance guard of mounted infantry had run into our rear in the narrow road, or opening in the forest, through which we were travelling; a fight or skirmish had taken place, and although they were driven back, they had killed a good many of our men. Later on I discovered that our rear had been allowed to straggle in the rain, and that several of the stragglers had been cut off and taken prisoners. A council of officers had been held during the night, and they had decided to wait for the enemy, and while apparently flying before him, allow him to come up, and give him battle; and with this object in view, we were hurrying forward to select our ground and make it as strong as possible. Away we went down the road as fast as the horses we rode could carry us, and we soon reached a hollow, where the water was rushing through from the recent heavy rains. The ground here was more open and free from brushwood, and we halted for a few minutes while Ryan examined the place; but after a few minutes' survey, he decided that it was unsuitable, so we crossed the stream and galloped ahead again, the ground rising as we advanced. After an hour's ride we came to a place that was considered satisfactory by our commander, and the men were dismounted and the horses unbitted, and calling on me, and a young Cuban who acted as guide, to follow him, he rode on ahead to examine the country.

About a mile from where we left the men we

reached the crest of the hill, from which there was a fine view of the country beyond. Although the wood extended for some distance down the slope, it had been getting more and more open from the point where we left the men, until it ended altogether about half-way down the hill from which we were looking; from thence there extended a fine stretch of open, rolling country; and beyond it, and as far all round as we could see, a beautiful parklike country, dotted all over with trees, lay spread out before us; while farther away rose the mountain ranges, getting fainter and more indistinct until they faded away altogether.

Ryan remained here a few minutes examining the country, and perhaps enjoying the beauty of the scenery, and after a short conversation with the Cuban, he wheeled his horse round and galloped back, the Cuban and I following, to where the men were left. No time was lost in preparing the ground. A point was chosen where some large trees grew close to the road on both sides, and the trees were cut nearly through, in such a way that they would fall across the road. A ditch was opened from near this point on the left-hand side of the road, and running away from it at an angle of forty-five degrees for a length of about sixty yards, then it bent and ran along about two hundred yards further, and parallel to the road, and running in the direction from which the enemy would have to approach. The brushwood, or undergrowth, was cut in the rear of the ditch, and arranged in front of it so as to form an abattis and mask the ditch, but there were openings left at intervals that were only slightly masked by a few branches that could be easily removed, to allow the defenders to go through and rush on the enemy. The ditch, where it ran parallel to the road, was not more than thirty or forty yards from it, and to any one coming along the road there was nothing to indicate that there had been any preparation made, or any defensive works thrown up. On the other side of the road, opposite the ditch, the undergrowth was so close that it would be impossible to leave the road on that side without cutting through it, and the ground sloped from that side down towards the ditch.

It was no easy task for us to cut the ditch. It was not continuous, but was broken here and there by the tough roots of trees that ran across it, and in some places it was only a series of short pits. In digging it our captain directed us to pass over the large roots, and not to lose time in cutting them, but continue the work where we could, so as not to delay; and then, when the work was well forward and near completion, we could, if there was time, cut through the roots and connect the different pits, and so make the ditch continuous;

but it was never done. We worked hard all day at it with very little rest; and the horses were not idle, either, for they were sent back to enable the remainder of our force to hurry forward. They began to arrive late in the afternoon, and it was dark before the last of them came in; but as soon as the last horse and wheeled vehicle passed, the trees were felled that blocked the road, and a ditch was cut across it, and obstacles placed in front and at the sides of it. The carts were drawn off the road into the wood, to a place prepared for them, and masked with brushwood

It was late when all this work was finished; but our company was allowed to light fires before nightfall, and prepare a meal of plantains and coffee, and we fared better than the others. As soon as the men had had something to eat, they were placed in the positions the commander intended that they should occupy, and all dogs were ordered to be destroyed, and strict silence kept, so that the enemy should not be made aware of our dispositions; and Ashton lost his pet—the little dog that gave us warning of the approach of the Spanish scout the day before, had to be destroyed with the others.

Fernandez and Morales, with their Cubans, occupied the wood to the rear of the barricade on the road, and the oblique part of the ditch; while Hudson, Wingate, and Ryan manned the remaining portion, and strict silence was enjoined on every one. Our position was on the right, or toward the farther end of the ditch, but at the extreme end the *picada*, or road, approached the ditch in a line almost perpendicular to it, to within forty yards, then turned and ran along parallel with it for some two hundred yards, when the ditch gradually approached the road, meeting it a short distance to the rear of the barricade.

CHAPTER XI.

Thunder, lightning, and rain—Sitting in a wet ditch—The enemy—A trying situation—Battle in the forest—Enemy beaten—Two guns captured—Prisoners shot.

ALTHOUGH we did not expect the enemy to appear before the forenoon of the next day, his advance guard might be close up with us before morning, and we were kept under arms and in our positions all night. No smoking, no talking, and no fires were allowed; even the sentries did not challenge, and signs with the hands and arms were substituted instead. Our company had worked hard all day; the gallop in the morning, and the spade and axe work all the rest of the day, left us in a state that we could sleep anywhere and on anything. Luckily for me, I had no sentry duty to perform that night, for I don't know how I could have kept my eyes open. I had no sooner sat down in the ditch with my back against the side of it, and a corner of my blanket thrown across my face to keep the mosquitoes off, than I was fast asleep, and I believe most of the others were in the same condition.

Some time in the night heavy thunder and lightning, followed by rain, came on, and woke us up; the ditch was soon filled with water, and there was no more sleep to be had, and we passed a miserable time, but as the Spanish proverb has it, "No hay mal que por bien no venga" (There is no misfortune but brings good in its train). Before daylight the flashes of lightning revealed to us plainly four of the enemy's mounted men coming along the road. No one challenged them, but they were reported to our commander, if he had not seen them himself, for every one was awake and on the alert, standing in the ditch with the water over his knees, or sitting on the edge of it in the mud, with his legs in the water. Every flash of lightning showed them plainly enough, even to their features, but not long enough to allow a man to take aim at them, for every flash was followed by a blinding darkness. Many a time I found myself passing my hand over my eyes, and rubbing them, and thinking for the moment that I had been struck blind with the lightning. The enemy rode along the road without let or hindrance, and passed out of our sight, going towards the barricade, and we listened and watched the flashes, to see if there were many more of them coming. We knew that the men who rode past us could not pass the barricade on horseback, and they would have to cut an opening in the brushwood to enable them to pass to the right of it; while if they attempted to pass to the left, they would have to cut away our abattis, or brushwood, in front of the ditch, and come in collision with our fellows. No more of the enemy appeared on the road as far as we could see by the lightning, and we knew that by this time the four we had seen ride past must have reached the barricade, and we were beginning to speculate as to what had become of them, when the lightning showed two of them riding back along the road again. I afterwards learned from some of the men who were up near the barricade, that when the four Spaniards reached it, and found the road obstructed, two of them dismounted to examine it, and climbed over it and examined the road on the other side, and the bush on each side of the road, as well as they could by the flashes of lightning, but found nothing, and they probably concluded that we were further ahead, and had obstructed the road to delay their march; for they got up on the barricade and sat down there after a conversation with the two who remained mounted. These were the two men we saw coming back; the other two remained sitting on the barricade until the rain drove them to take shelter near some trees. Not long after this we heard a noise of horses on the road, but could see nothing, as the lightning ceased, and the rain was coming down in torrents. The noise increased, and we could hear them, not only on the road, but in among the trees on our side of it between the road and the ditch, where the forest was most open. After a while the lightning began to flash again, and we got momentary glimpses of them. The road was crowded with mounted men, and there were a good many amongst the trees, and they seemed undecided what to do, for as the head of the column was up at the barricade, and obliged to halt, while they still pressed on from the rear, the men had to turn off the road wherever they found standing room, and the lightning showed us the road and the whole space in front of us crowded with troops, and at the bend of the road we saw some artillery halted.

As we sat in our wet ditch, we heard them talking and pulling the brushwood about close to us, and whenever a flash of lightning came, we saw them so near to us that we could almost reach over and touch them with our rifles. They were scattered about under the trees without any kind of order, and only for the brushwood in our front, would have tumbled into the ditch on top of us. We were greatly excited, for the least noise might warn the enemy of our presence.

I have often wondered since that none of our horses neighed in answer to the enemy's, for *they* made noise enough. True, ours were taken away some distance into the forest beyond the barricade, but still not so far but that they could have been easily heard by a watchful enemy. The Cubans who were in charge of them may have known of some way of preventing it, although I am doubtful if covering their heads would be of any use. The discomforts of our position and predicament — up to our middles in mud and water, with the rain pouring down on us—was at the moment unfelt in our excitement and eagerness in watching the enemy. Little Jos Storey, who was next to me, grasped my arm excitedly, and whispered in my ear, while trembling all over: "Oh! what will I do? I can't help it. I must scream, or fire off my rifle." I was afraid that he would do either one or the other, and I whispered back in his ear: "Storey, if you make the least noise, I'll stab you to death," although, of course, nothing was farther from my intentions; but it was the first thing that occurred to me to say, and I was really afraid that he would make a noise. I then told him to keep his eyes closed, and try and think about something else, until he heard the first shot fired, and after that he might shout as loud as he liked; and to soothe him, I put one arm round his neck, and drew him close up against me, where he rested like a child, trembling all over. I was afraid that he might go into a fit, and I kept my arm round him until the excitement wore off, which it gradually did, as he became accustomed to the situation; and then, I think, he felt ashamed of himself, for he begged of me not to say anything about it to any of the men, and I never spoke of it after, not even to my friend Ashton.

The reader must not think badly of Storey for this, or fancy that he was cowardly in any way; on the contrary, although he was but a slight-built, girlish-looking lad, there was not a braver man in the expedition, and although like a child in some things, he was a gallant little soul in action. I could make allowances for Storey, for I was not free from the feeling myself; but I was able to master it, and from the moment that I put my arm round him it left me altogether, and I became as cool and firm as a rock. Our position was very trying to young, untrained soldiers; I think it would be so even to veterans—sitting for hours in a wet ditch, within touch and hearing of an immensely superior enemy, superior in numbers, discipline, and equipment, and waiting quietly for daylight to begin the fight.

Sometimes the rain would cease altogether, and everything be still for a few minutes, when one could almost hear the breathing of the men. Then some one would make a splash in the ditch farther along, or you could hear an "ahem!" or a stifled cough, until one wondered how the enemy did not hear us. Luckily for us, the lulls in the rain only lasted a few minutes. How we longed for it to come down! We no longer felt the discomfort of it, for the noise it made falling on the leaves of the trees drowned any sounds made by our men, and if, in the lulls, the enemy's men did hear anything, they must have attributed it to the noises made by their own people, we were so close to one another. Another thing also helped us, they spoke amongst themselves, and uttered maledictions on us, and on the weather; but the rain and storm that night were our best friends, and believing that we were some distance on the road ahead of them, they only thought of sheltering themselves from the weather, otherwise they could never have allowed themselves to get huddled up in such a *cul-de-sac* as we had prepared for them.

At dawn of day they began to remove the obstructions on the road, and that precipitated the fight. The Cubans manned the barricade, and opened a deadly fire on them at close quarters. There was scarcely light to see on the road, and where our company was posted in the wood it was still dark. The enemy were astonished at first, but they quickly brought forward two guns, and unlimbered and pointed them in the direction of the barricade. They were on the road, right in front of our position; one of them a little in the rear of the other, as there was not room to work both together in the narrow road; and the enemy's men, who were between them and the barricade, got off the road and amongst the trees out of the line of fire. All was yet quiet along the ditch; not a sound was heard from any of us, but we expected every moment to get the order to open fire. The firing was going on rapidly up at the barricade; the enemy were replying to our men from behind the trees, and the shot from the two guns on the road in front of us was tearing and crashing through the barricade, and still we remained silent in our wet ditch; but as the daylight comes rapidly in the tropics, we soon had light enough to see that they were in a terrible mess. Horses and men were crowded together in a confused mob among the trees between the road and the ditch, and we were surprised that we were not ordered to attack, for we could now see them plainly. At last the order came, and it was another surprise to the enemy. If we had had repeating arms in those days, not a man would have escaped. They fell back precipitately towards the road, and all who could sought shelter behind the trees, and some of them returned our fire. They crowded so thickly about the guns that their artillerymen could not work them, and while the pandemonium lasted, amidst the shouts and oaths of the men, and the officers trying to ride through them and rally them, we poured in a merciless fire on them. After a little time they got the guns cleared again, and one of them was wheeled round a little, so as to take the oblique part of the ditch, and we now saw two more guns beyond the bend of the road, unlimbered and pointed in our direction.

The first volley from our men in the ditch unmasked all our positions, but the enemy had only fired one shot from these guns, when our bugles sounded the advance, and Ryan called to us: "Now, boys, draw swords, follow me, and hurrah for the guns!" We could hear Wingate's voice shouting further along on our left, calling on his men to hurry on, and to remember that there was to be no quarter.

The brushwood that masked the alley-ways in the abattis was dragged in, and we rushed through the openings, and the next moment were on the enemy, cutting and slashing right and left among them. Our rush was so fierce and so unexpected that a panic seized them, and they gave way and fled at once. Those who were mounted fled helter-skelter without looking behind them, trampling and riding over their own men, and even knocking each other over in the narrow roadway in their hurry to get away. Some of the Spanish artillerymen stuck to their guns to the last, and in the fight round them, one of our fellows was engaged with an artilleryman, but the Spaniard, being a better swordsman, after a few parries ran our man through with his sword, and he dropped dead near me. When the Spaniard turned to fly, instead of running him through the back, as I might have done, I jumped forward and grappled with him, and we both rolled over in the mud together. In a moment he had me under him, and planting a knee on each arm, he held me firmly down in the mud, and was shortening his point to run me through, when Captain Wingate came charging along with his men, and gave the artilleryman a kick on the jaw that must have broken it, for it lifted him off me, and as he rolled over on his back, even before I had time to rise, one of Wingate's men ran him through with his bayonet.

When I got on my feet, I found the men of my company round the guns, and trying to drag them back by hand, for the horses had disappeared with the retreating enemy; and I joined in with them, and we hauled one gun back over the muddy road, and got it into position at the bend, and opened fire down the road, on the retreating and demoralised enemy.

They managed to get away with the two rear guns and the ammunition waggons, and they must have left early in the fight, for they were out of sight down the road when we reached the bend; but we worked the gun while there was a man of them to be seen, and until Morales and another Cuban officer got round the horses, and with all the mounted men that could be mustered, went in pursuit of them; Wingate with his infantry following and searching the wood on each side of the road. Between the bend in the road and the barricade there were a good many horses, living and dead; the living ones were wounded horses, for Morales had taken any sound ones that were there, to mount his men in pursuit of the enemy.

I recollected that, when we were dragging the gun along, there appeared to be several of the enemy still fighting between us and the barricade. They were surrounded by our men, and now that we had a moment's breathing time to look about us in broad daylight, we saw that they were prisoners —unfortunate wretches!—and Fernandez was in the act of having them shot. He treated them exactly as the Spaniards treated his countrymen, whenever any of them fell into their hands; and we felt little pity for them when we learnt that some of our men, who had been captured two days before by the enemy in his attack on our rear, had been summarily shot by order of the Spanish commander.

CHAPTER XII.

Death of Ridley—Pursuit of enemy—Capture of waggons—
March on San Jacinto—Assault and capture of San
Jacinto—I am wounded—Capture of horses and mules—
Promoted.

As the morning advanced the rain cleared away, and we attended to our wounded. We had over twenty, but few of them seriously, and we lost in killed nine or ten. As for the enemy, I could not tell his loss—there were no prisoners and no wounded. I counted seventy-two dead between our gun at the bend of the road and the barricade, and beyond the bend, away down the road as far as one could see, they lay in little groups of two and three. Colonel Ridley died some time during the night, no one could tell when, for when they went to tell him the result of the fight in the morning, they found him dead in the little cart that served him for a bed, with the rain beating down on his uncovered face. But he was not the only one; three more of the sick died some time between night and morning.

When Morales returned from the pursuit of the enemy, he reported them completely broken up and dispersed. He was unable to overtake the two guns or the ammunition waggons; but he said that he finished every Spaniard that he met on the road or overtook. He captured two waggons with provisions. When the drivers found him closing on them, they took out the horses and mules, and made their escape on them, abandoning the waggons on the road. Morales' men refreshed themselves from the contents of the waggons, and setting one of them on fire, they contrived to drag the other with their lazos back to camp, where the contents were distributed amongst the men. The share that fell to my lot consisted of three biscuits and a piece of soap, all very acceptable at the time, and we feasted that night on horse-flesh and biscuit.

Horse-flesh is not such bad feeding after all, particularly when one has been without meat of any kind for some days, and, indeed, it is almost as good as the beef one gets in Cuba. We found the tongue and the *loma,* or meat along by the back-bone, the tenderest parts; but very little flesh meat satisfies a man in the tropics, when he can get other food.

Nearly all the enemy's dead wore the uniform of the regular Spanish troops; but the Cubans who went in pursuit of them told us that there were a great many volunteers, natives of old Spain, in the forces that were opposed to us, and that the enemy that morning outnumbered us three to one. We buried Colonel Ridley and our own dead in the afternoon, and shifted camp to fresh ground over the crest of the hill, so as to be away from the enemy's dead, and we slept well the night after the fight, and rested all the following day. Messengers were sent ahead to inform the revolutionary junta of our success, and to spread the news of our victory over the country. Several Cubans joined us here, and our little army began to swell in numbers, provisions were sent to us, and promises of horses were made; so true is it that "nothing succeeds like success." The victorious soldier, like the successful civilian, will always find friends to sound his praises, or lend him money; while the poor beaten wretch, let his struggle be ever so gallant in the field, or deserving in his calling, is shunned and disparaged by everybody. As we had no ammunition for the captured guns but what we found in the limbers, one was dismounted and hidden away in the woods, and we managed to horse the other, and took it with us.

After the check that the enemy had received, our leaders concluded that he would not be in a hurry to follow us up again for some time, at any rate until he had collected a much larger force; in the meantime, if we could gain another success, the whole country round would flock to join us. We were told of a place named San Jacinto, where there was a Government *caballada,* or troop of horses, in charge of a small garrison, and although it was not in our line of march, we determined to make a deviation and take it, as we were badly in want of horses, and those we had were pretty well done up.

After a day and a night's march, we found ourselves close to it in the morning before breakfast, and no time was lost in reconnoitring, for at eight in the morning our attack was delivered. As one of the rank and file, I cannot say what the plan of attack was, and I only know what took place in my own vicinity. My company advanced without check until we found ourselves at a ditch; the soil was loose and sandy, and we dropped into it, and found no difficulty in scaling the scarp on the opposite side. I was young and active, blessed with good health, and eager to distinguish myself, and was one of the first to scale the ditch and reach the berm, which was very narrow, and crumbled away under our feet. With rifle slung across my back, and my sword held between my teeth, so as to enable me to use both hands in climbing, I raised my face for a moment to look above me, and saw a Spanish soldier standing over me, with his musket clubbed and uplifted, in the act of aiming a blow at me. I was powerless to defend myself; I might have avoided the blow by letting go with my hands and feet and dropping into the ditch, but that would look like running away, and somehow I felt as if it were all over with me. A tremendous crash on the head, the sight left my eyes, a sense of falling, and I knew no more.

When consciousness returned, I recollected everything, how I had been struck on the head, and knew that I was lying at the bottom of the ditch. I felt something moist in one of my eyes, and remembering distinctly the blow I had received, I wondered how I was alive. I thought that my skull was crushed in from the force of the blow, and although still alive and conscious, it was the consciousness before death, and the least movement of my body would precipitate it; and yet I felt a strong desire to put up my hand and feel my head, and ascertain the extent of the damage. Just then I heard some one beside me talking to me. It was Ashton, who was asking me if I was badly hurt; and getting an arm under me, he raised me into a sitting posture.

I said no, although I did not know at the time whether I was or not, but I thought it was the proper thing to say, even if one were dying; and putting my hand up, I found my skull still to the good, and that I was bleeding from a wound on the scalp, and the blood was running into my eyes, and with Ashton's assistance I got out of the ditch. Our company was the most unfortunate, and suffered most, for where we attacked was the only place where there was a ditch. Wingate's company, who were on our right, marched right in without finding any impediment. It appeared that the enemy began the ditch with the intention of carrying it round the village, but afterwards they considered it unnecessary, and never finished it. They fought well, but they were outnumbered and driven pell-mell out of the place, and we captured the greater part of the *caballada*, or horse troop, together with some mules in very good condition. We lost Lanoy, a lieutenant, Smith, a sergeant, and seven men killed, three of them Cubans, and we had a good many wounded. That evening I was made sergeant.

CHAPTER XIII.

San Jacinto—Spanish roofs—Fernandez leaves us with one of the guns—Ditching—Shower-baths—Spanish troops—Besieged—Dig out old guns—Mounting gun on church tower—Enemy reconnoitring—We drive them back—We open fire—Gun bursts.

SAN JACINTO was a little dilapidated place with from forty to fifty habitable houses, and consisted of two *plazas*, or squares, separated by the priest's house and the church. The squares were not all built on, and there was only a house here and there around them. The grass and trees grew in the squares, and round the houses and the church in every direction. There were not two good houses in the place, and the only inhabitants were a few mulattoes. The houses, such as they were, had been occupied by the Spanish soldiery.

The church was a small building with two towers, or rather the builders intended that it should have two, but one had never been finished, and the other served for a belfry. The upper part of it, where the bell hung, was open at the sides, but covered over with a dome of masonry, supported by short square pillars at the corners; it was the only building with an *Azotea* roof, a style of roof peculiar to Spanish countries. It is a flat, or nearly flat, roof, with only sufficient slope to allow the rain to run off, and is built thus: Beams or joists of hard wood, or palm-trees, are laid from wall to wall, at distances of about eighteen inches apart, the dimensions of the beams or palms depending on the span of the roof; across these beams are laid strong battens of hard wood, inch, or inch and a half, by about three inches, at such a distance one from another, that a brick laid lengthways will rest on two contiguous battens, bridging over the space between them, and the whole roof is covered over with bricks laid in this manner; then on the bricks is spread a layer of mortar, and another layer of bricks is bedded in this mortar, breaking joint with the first layer. Next another coat of mortar is laid on, in which a layer of smooth, square, flat tiles are bedded and closely jointed, and the roof is complete, and makes a clean, safe, and airy place to sleep or walk about on in the hot tropical nights. In private houses there is a low wall or balustrade built on top around the front of the buildings, and ornamented with stucco balusters, or short pilasters are built along the front at intervals of a few yards, and the intervening space filled in with a wrought-iron railing; this serves as an adornment, and also allows the inmates to lean on it and look over into the streets below. I may state here that the bricks used are not shaped like English bricks, but like those used in Spain and Spanish America, and are about twelve inches long by six inches wide, and one and a half or two inches thick.

On one side of the village ran a little stream, and we were no sooner installed in the place than every one enjoyed the luxury of a good wash, both their bodies and their clothing; and we were put to work at making the ditch that the enemy had begun, and kept at it all day without resting, and by nightfall it was finished, and the little village completely shut in. Only two openings were left. From this we began to suspect that it was decided to remain here for some time, instead of marching on at once now that we had horses. The next morning we were joined by some Cuban leaders, and after a consultation with our officers, they left the same evening with Comandante Fernandez and three hundred of the best mounted men, taking also the captured gun and twenty men of our artillery company; Hodson, who was next in command to Ridley, remaining in command at San Jacinto, but Hodson was sick and weak, and Ryan was virtually the commander.

We were divided into fatigue parties, and used to relieve each other every day, in doing something to the ditch of circumvallation, widening and deepening it, until it began to look quite formidable. There were all kinds of rumours flying about among the men as to the object of this work. Some had it that a strong force of Cubans were expected with artillery, and that they would return with Fernandez, and guns would be mounted, and the place made head-quarters for the patriot army, and that recruits were to concentrate there; others, who knew better, told them that there could be no intention to mount guns, or Ryan, who was our engineer as well as our artillery officer, would have set them to work to prepare timber for the platforms; besides, the ditches were made too close to the houses. The horses and mules were all fed outside; although there was grass growing in the plazas, the animals were not allowed to touch it, but were driven out early every morning under a guard, and men were sent out every evening to cut grass and bring it in, so that they could have a ration of grass in the night when they were tied up to pickets round the church; besides this, great piles of grass were brought in and dried, and stacked in the church, and we were not allowed to pull the plantains, or fruit that grew in and around the place; but parties were sent every day on horseback to forage the country round for our supplies. Some of us thought it very hard at the time, to be made to ride for miles in a hot sun, or a pelting rain—for it rained three or four times a week—in search for what we had close at hand, near the village, and in the plaza itself; but we afterwards learnt the wisdom of it. Nearly all the houses for leagues round the village were deserted, and many of them burnt down by the Spanish soldiery, as they were owned by insurgents, or people favourable to their cause, and their plantations had been trampled down by the Government troopers; but for all that, owing to the constant rains and the heat, everything was growing luxuriously wild, and in our daily forays we brought in vegetables and fruits of all kinds; but no cattle were to be seen anywhere. We had a notion, somehow—I don't know how it got hold of us, but we believed that it was necessary to have flesh meat occasionally, to keep up our strength, and some mules were butchered now and again, as they were in much better condition than the horses; and another reason, I think, was, that we had taken a dislike to the mules. Soup was made from the flesh; but still our sick men got no better, and scarcely a day passed that we had not to bury some one; they were principally the youngest who succumbed.

My face and head were swelled and sore from

the blow I had received on the day of the attack, and I was never free from pain when I was on horseback; the motion of the horse in galloping or trotting made me feel as if every bone in my head was loose, and shaking together, although on the afternoon of the day on which I received it, I went into the ditch with the others, and worked until night to finish it. I am free to confess now, that I was not fit for the work, and it was done merely out of bravado, for I was in agony, and almost blind with pain, while I worked all that afternoon; and considering the state I was in, working under a tropical sun with my head uncovered most of the time, I am amazed to think how I escaped. It is surprising, sometimes, what youngsters will go through and escape scathless.

A little distance above the village, the brook that flowed past it tumbled over a bank of soft red sandstone, about sixteen or eighteen feet high, but instead of falling in one continuous sheet of water, it was split up into half-a-dozen little rills, each one of which had eaten out a horse-shoe shape for itself in the bank, and fell into a little circular basin, that was shut in by the sides of the bank all round, and the only entrance to it was through the opening where the water flowed out to join the stream, and each one formed a natural shower-bath in a little grotto; the trees growing on each side above, shaded the whole place, and made it a delightfully cool spot to bathe and rest in.

A few days after our arrival, some of the men noticed that the few women who remained in the village, went away up-stream to fill their water jars, instead of filling them at the stream close by; and following them, they found them at the place described, where, after filling their jars, they went into the baths that nature had provided for them, and were enjoying themselves in the water. Ashton had been there with the others, and brought the news to me, saying that "the water was delightfully cool, just the thing for you, 'twill cure your head right away. Come along, I'll show you the way."

I went with him and found it all that it was described. The water was scarcely more than two feet deep in the little basin where I went in, and one could only lie down in it and enjoy the refreshing coolness after coming out of the glaring hot sun. But I was foolish enough to be persuaded by my friend Ashton to stand under the falling stream, as he said "it's just the thing to fix you properly, and take down that swelling."

Yes, it did "fix me properly," sure enough! The shock of the falling waters on my head knocked me senseless, and Ashton had to drag me out of the water. A mulatto woman who happened to come for water or to bathe herself, seeing what had happened, ran back for a remedy, and when I came to my senses, I was lying on the sand in the little grotto at the water's edge, with my head on the woman's lap, who was chafing my head and face with cocoa-nut oil. Ashton was standing by watching the operation. I don't know if the cocoa-nut oil did me any good, but it was the most valuable thing that the poor creature possessed, and is often used as a remedy for various ailments. With all the care of Ashton and the woman, it was over an hour before I could attempt to dress and walk back to the village, and I had to keep quiet for a couple of days after this. About a week afterwards I was out with the horse guard pasturing the horses; our orders were, that in the event of seeing anything suspicious, men or animals, moving about, we were to round up the *caballada* immediately, and drive them towards the village without waiting for orders; and we were not to allow the horses to scatter too much, but there was no restriction as to distance, the guard always keeping outside the horses. The horse guard drove out the horses early in the morning, and remained with them all day, returning with them at nightfall. There were usually about twenty to twenty-five men in the guard, and some of them took a few bananas with them as food for the day, but they mostly depended on what they could pick up outside. An officer with two orderlies visited the *caballada* twice during the day, a little before the siesta hour, and a short time after it, to see that all was well, for the horse guard was not allowed to sleep siesta.

There was a hill about two leagues distant from us that I felt a longing to go up and look out from, and see what the country was like beyond it, and I often spoke of it to Ashton, but he had no inclination to go there, and used to say: "Oh, I don't see any good in a fellow tiring himself and his horse by going up there for nothing. You may be sure there is nothing more to be seen there than we can see from here. It's all the same kind of country." But this day we happened to be on that side, and nearer to the hill than usual, and I proposed to Storey that we should ride to it and have a look at the country on the other side. Storey was delighted, and wanted to be off at once, but I had to wait until the officer passed on his round in the afternoon; and then as everything seemed all right, we started full gallop for the hill. When we had ridden half-way up we had to pull in to ease our horses, as they were pretty well blown with their gallop, and then we saw that if we went any further in that direction, we would in all probability be seen from San Jacinto, for we recollected that the officers were continually looking with their glasses at the country all round, and near the top of this hill there were no trees or bushes of any kind; so when we got to where the trees finished, we skirted them round to get on the other side of the hill. It was fatiguing work both for ourselves and our horses, but we accomplished it at last, and sat down to rest awhile before climbing again. We did not delay long, and started again to go up, leading the horses by the bridles, but it began to get too steep for the horses, and we tied them together and hobbled one of them, and climbed to the top, where we sat down once more and rested, enjoying the nice cool breeze that made it feel as if we were in another climate altogether.

We had a good view of the surrounding country from where we sat. Before us were several ranges of hills, mostly covered with forest up to their summits, but although we could see open savannas and water in several places, we could not detect any sign of cultivation. Not an animal of any kind was to be seen, nor any sign of life. Up here we were free from mosquitoes and other pests that swarmed amongst the trees below, and round San Jacinto. Looking over the brow of the hill behind us we could see our quarters and the village looking very pretty and peaceful in the trees, and we could catch glimpses of the horses as they moved about in the open places outside to feed, but there was no other sign of life anywhere. Away to the northwest we could see the mountains blue and indistinct, and Storey said, pointing towards them :

"I suppose the principal fighting is going on over there; Fernandez with his crowd will be yonder. I wonder what in thunder we are hanging on here for?" I wondered also. "There ain't no Spaniards nor anybody else, unless Indians, in these woods, or we'd see smoke, and there's nothing to prevent us from marching right away over there to join the main body. Eh, boss, what do you think?"

I did not tell him all I thought, for I was beginning to think that we were the main body ourselves; but I told him that I believed that there were no Indians in the woods, nor had there been for the last two hundred years; they had died out long ago, or intermarried with the Spaniards, and their descendants were to be found in some of the Cubans who were with us. Both my companion and myself would have liked to go on exploring the woods and country before us, if time and circumstances would allow it; but we had to hurry back to get inside the ditch before nightfall, and had to take some care that we did not lose our way. When we reached the horses and untied them, we led them in a contour line round the hill to the opposite side, and then mounted and started for home, although this was a needless precaution, as we learned afterwards, for if we had given the horses their heads, they would have brought us back by the shortest way to their companions in the troop.

A few days after this, news arrived that Fernandez and his party had fallen in with superior forces of the enemy, and had suffered a reverse, and that the junta and the insurgent forces in the mountains were defeated and dispersed; but we could not learn whether Fernandez himself had been killed or captured. But two days after the receipt of this news, a Spanish force appeared in front of us, too numerous for us, with our reduced numbers, to attack in the open with any probability of success. They appeared about midday, driving in our horse guard and horses before them, and we found ourselves shut in in San Jacinto.

There was no more going out in the morning to feed the horses, or to forage for food for ourselves. Now we knew what we had been widening and deepening the ditches for, and what we had been cutting and saving grass for. There were no more cool baths to be had, morning and evening, up at the grottoes; but it was stand to arms all day and all night. The enemy reconnoitred our position; probably he knew it well, as the force we drove out when we took it was with him, and

I suppose he satisfied himself that we were well entrenched, for he did not attack, but contented himself with watching us for two or three days; but we were not idle in the meantime. We dug out two old iron guns that were stuck in the ground for posts. They were short, like a ship's carronades, very rusty and honey-combed, and one of them was useless, as the muzzle was broken off; but the other we cleaned up and made a carriage, or rather a sled, to mount it on, out of a mahogany log which we found; and as it was to be mounted on the church tower, the men were engaged in getting everything ready to work it.

The tower was measured, and some of the men were put to work to prepare logs for a floor or platform, out of whatever timber could be had from the houses; others were employed in preparing ammunition. The bell was got down out of the tower and broken up; and every scrap of metal about the place was collected, to be used as shot against the enemy.

Some men were sent to the little stream, where it ran past the village, and was commanded by our fire, to collect all the roundest stones and pebbles that they could find.

The cupola of brickwork over the tower was cracked, and it was thought advisable to get rid of it to prevent its coming down on our heads at the first discharge of the gun; so some holes were made in it and charged with powder, and fired, blowing away the half of it, but the remaining portion, although separated from the columns that supported it and moved out, still rested on them, and hung there undecided whether to fall in or out.

We had to go up with wedges and levers, and after half an hour's work we succeeded in toppling it over. It canted in falling, and fell partly on the wall and on the roof, and although some of the timbers were broken, it did not go through. Meanwhile the enemy watched us while we worked at the tower, from the shelter of a clump of trees that grew nearer to the ditch than was desirable; and on hearing the noise of the explosion and the falling masonry, some of his officers came out from under the trees, and with glass in hand, stood watching us while we prised over the blocks of masonry with our levers. Ryan, seeing this, sent some of the best shots among the men out as sharpshooters, with orders to get outside the ditch on the opposite side, and creep round and down as close as possible to them before firing; they were not to fall back if attacked, but hold their ground, and there was a reserve told off, and posted in the ditch to support them. They were to do all they could to draw the enemy out of the trees, as Ryan wanted to find out their strength.

Lieutenants Burney and Jackson were in command of them, while the rest of us worked away as hard as we could to get the gun ready, as if there was nothing else on hand for the moment. Burney managed to get within easy range before they discovered what was going on, and they were just about making a movement to get under the cover of the trees when our fellows fired on them, dropping a good many of them.

Looking from the church tower where I was at the time, our skirmishers seemed to be quite close to the Spanish officers when they opened fire on them. They advanced and entered the trees, where we lost sight of them, and the firing began again. The supports were ordered forward, and the firing went on in the trees, but we could see nothing except a movement amongst the enemy in the open to the left rear of the trees, where our men had entered. Ryan was on the tower watching with his glass, but as he could not see what was going on, he ordered the retreat to be sounded, and soon after our men appeared, coming out of the trees, carrying bundles of all kinds, clothing, uniforms, wine, and preserves, and several other articles. They came back unpursued by the enemy, and I heard one fellow say that night that they could have gone right through the whole Spanish camp if they had not been recalled; but the fellow was half-drunk with wine that he brought from the Spanish tents, and his statement was of little value.

From what I could learn from the men who took part in the skirmish, our men had advanced some distance through the trees before they came on any of the enemy, with the exception of the officers who were out in front, who fell back before them, our fellows driving them up to and past some tents, which they found pitched under some trees, and pursued them a little distance beyond the tents when they were recalled. They rummaged the tents, which proved to be officers' tents, and brought away everything that they could carry with them.

Burney reported that he found two officers of rank lying dead just inside the trees from the first fire, and he believed that of the others who got away, most of them were wounded. We had only three men wounded; of course we could not tell what the enemy's loss was from the firing in the trees, or if he suffered any loss besides the two officers that Burney saw, and of which there could be no doubt, for our fellows stripped them coming back, and brought in their swords and uniforms. Next morning our gun was ready on the tower, and we opened fire with it on where we thought the enemy's head-quarters were situated among the trees. We fired everything we had at them, stones, pieces of the broken church bell, iron bolts, and crowbars cut in short pieces, and our fire must have annoyed them, for by midday we saw some of their tents moved to the rear.

In the evening our old gun burst, after firing forty-two rounds. The whole chase, from the trunnions to the muzzle, blew out, and although there were five of us round it at the time, no one was hurt; it blew forward with the charge without doing any harm.

CHAPTER XIV.

The enemy attack—They fall back—They attack again—Repulse of the enemy—Out at night looking for food—Astray—Spanish sentries—Going to die—Thoughts of home—I get my bananas—Get back safely.

On the afternoon of the third day the enemy advanced as if with the intention of attacking us, but after half an hour's desultory firing, they fell back without doing anything; but that same night we were informed that we would be attacked at daybreak next morning. I don't know where the news came from, but it turned out perfectly correct. Indeed, we were always kept well informed of the movements and intentions of the enemy whenever he was near us by some means or another, probably by spies or sympathisers; and we also remarked that when the odds were much against us, our Cuban companions diminished in number, but they fought well while they were with us.

In the evening we were distributed along the ditch sparsely, with a reserve in the *plaza*, as we did not know where the attack would be made. We expected to be attacked at several points at the same time so as to confuse us, and on finding out our weakest point, the enemy would concentrate all the force that he could and push it home. That, I suppose, is the usual tactic in war, but our enemy on this occasion did not think it worth while to do so. He made too sure of us, and attacked at break of day in two columns, coming straight up to one point, his men carrying planks to enable them to cross the ditch. After a sharp contest he was compelled to fall back, leaving a good many of his men dead outside the ditch and on the slope beyond it. One officer and two men carrying a plank had actually reached the ditch, but fell dead into it.

Young as I was, I could not help thinking that, although we took credit to ourselves and prided ourselves on repulsing the enemy, if his attack had been made with a more extended front, he would have succeeded in forcing an entrance; or if he had attacked at two points, as we had not sufficient force to man all our defences properly. He had men enough to do so, but luckily for us he did not; for had he succeeded, if we did not die fighting, we would have been shot or garroted before sundown as rebels and filibusters, and I would not now be writing these lines. Ashton, Storey, and I had often spoken about and considered that contingency, what would we do if we saw no escape from falling into the hands of the Spaniards as prisoners, and we had resolved not to be taken alive; there was something horrifying in the thought of being paraded out for execution. I always had my revolver on me, and I was told that the surest way of putting an end to oneself was to put the barrel in your mouth and hold it firmly with your teeth while you pull the trigger.

Since the arrival of the enemy, some of our men in their greed had appropriated all the fruit and vegetables growing inside and near the ditch, leaving the others with nothing but the horse and mules' flesh, that was served out as rations, with a little maize; but there were some fine plantains and bananas growing outside around the village that we had spared, intending to make use of them later on, but the sudden arrival of the Spaniards cut us off from them, and we found that we had been sparing them for the enemy, who were now encamped amongst them and enjoying them.

The night following the repulse of the Spaniards, I proposed to Ashton, Storey, and another, that we should slip out and try and procure some, and they eagerly assented. Poor little Storey! he was far from well at that time; but my proposal seemed to enliven him. I proposed to make the first attempt myself that night, and Storey wanted to go with me; but I would not allow him, for I thought it better that I should make the attempt alone.

Ashton was to light a little fire at the corner of the ditch where I went out, and keep it burning so as to guide me in coming back; otherwise I might go astray, or strike the ditch where the other sentries were posted.

I got out all right, and crept along on my face and hands directly towards the Spanish encampment until I thought I was out of sight and hearing of our own sentries; then I moved along parallel, as I thought, with the ditch, and while moving in that direction I stumbled over a dead body—one of the enemy who had fallen in the morning's fight. This little accident disconcerted me for a moment, and, perhaps, caused me unwittingly to alter my course. I had forgotten the fight in the morning, and it had escaped my calculation altogether that I might stumble over some of the dead in the dark, for there were several of the enemy's dead lying away outside the ditch. For a moment I was paralysed. The thought flashed through me that I had fallen into the hands of the enemy, some Spaniard who had intuitively become aware of my intention, and was waiting for me; and it was a wholesome relief to me to find that it was only a dead enemy instead of a living one. I moved along again, crouching low, until

I thought that I was about abreast of the enemy's flank. I then paused for a moment to make sure of my position, and to listen. All was silent. I looked back, but could not see Ashton's fire at the ditch where I came out. I could see the fires in the Spanish encampment plain enough, and people passing in front of them; but no sign of Ashton's fire. I could not tell exactly in what direction lay the point from which I started. In fact, I was completely astray—lost.

I recollected reading of some one getting lost in a wood, and the writer recommended that, in such cases, one should not get excited or run about looking for a road, tiring himself out to no purpose, and only making bad worse; that it was better to sit down quietly, and try to think what way you came, and how the wind was blowing when you started, and how you felt it on your head and face as you journeyed on, and that that might be a means of guiding you out of your difficulties. So I remained quiet for a short time, looking towards the enemy's camp, and anon towards where I thought our own lay, and trying to think out my position. After a while I raised myself on my legs and stood upright, and looked all round me. In a few moments I saw a little flame blaze up on my left, and then subside again, and presently it burned away steadily, as if it had been just lighted, or allowed to burn low, and had a fresh handful of fuel thrown on it; still, it was not in the direction in which I expected to see it, so that I was bewildered, and did not venture to move. I waited and watched the fire until I saw some twigs thrown on it from time to time, and then I felt sure that it was Ashton's fire, and yet it seemed twice as far away from where I stood as the Spanish camp; still, there could be no mistake about it, and I knew that I must hurry up and get back quickly, or Ashton might give up hope, thinking that I had fallen into the hands of the enemy, and let the fire go out. I took my bearings as carefully as I could. I turned my face round in every direction to try and find out how the wind was blowing, for it was a dark and cloudy night, and not a star was to be seen, and no wind—at least, none that I could feel, until I recollected what I had seen a sailor do in a calm at sea, when he wanted to find out if there was any light air stirring. I put a finger in my mouth for a moment to wet it, and held it over my head, and on feeling the back part grow cooler than the rest of it, I knew that what little wind there was, was blowing from me towards the Spanish camp. The theory is that the air blowing on the wet finger causes the moisture to evaporate more quickly on the side that it strikes against, and gives rise to a sensible coldness on that side.

I now felt great misgivings as to the success of my undertaking, and I was beginning to get doubtful that I was not hastening to my own destruction; however, if I wished to return, I had only to move along carefully, keeping the wind on my left cheek, and I would reach the point I had started from, or very near it, even if Ashton's fire went out; but I did not like the idea of going back without making the attempt.

I thought "fortune favours the bold," and throwing my fears to the wind, I started again, moving along swiftly and crouching low, towards the Spanish camp. The noises made by the frogs and the insects in a swamp close by favoured me. I had not gone very far when a loud " *Quien viva?* " alarmingly near stopped me. I could not make out where the sentry was posted who challenged, but I moved away to the right. He evidently heard me, for the challenge was repeated, and I, knowing what would follow, dropped on my face and hands, when—bang went his musket. I moved as fast as I could to the right, thinking that the Spanish guard would turn out, and they might advance in the expectation of some movement on our side, and our fellows might open fire on them so that I would be between two fires, and I hurried to get out of the way.

I soon found myself getting into swampy ground, and waited awhile to think and decide on my next move. I listened to hear of any movement on the enemy's side, but the noise of frogs around me prevented me from hearing anything else; and as I knew that there were no bananas to be had where I was, I moved on again towards the Spanish camp, guided by the glare from the fires that the enemy kept burning there. Suddenly the fires went out altogether, and Ashton's little fire was nowhere to be seen. I kept moving along mechanically towards where I thought I last saw them for a few minutes, but suddenly stopped short, as a sense of my perilous and helpless position forced itself on me. Where was I going to?

I judged that before the fires went out I was somewhere on the enemy's right, and rather to the rear. I again sat down to collect myself and decide on what to do. Surely, I thought, Ashton has his beacon fire burning, but it is hidden from me by the nature of the ground; and I started to my feet again and looked all around, but nothing was to be seen—not a light anywhere. I knew that unless I had something to guide me, that if I made any movement, it would be ten chances to one that I would walk into the hands of the enemy, for I now and again heard voices in Spanish, but they seemed to be all round me. I fancied that I had got into the middle of the Spanish camp, so I sat quietly on the ground waiting and watching for some sign to guide me, but none came. How long I remained in this position I don't know, it seemed hours to me, and I knew that I must soon do something. I debated in my mind whether it were better to walk on until I was shot or captured; wait where I sat until daylight to meet the same fate; or end my troubles there and then by my own hand. I could not bear the thought of being a prisoner. I knew well what to expect from the enemy: that I would be paraded before his men and publicly shot or garroted as a criminal.

Hope was leaving me. Was I to die there? I thought of my companions whom I had left of my own free will only a short while before—of my mother and my home in that other island, with four thousand miles of ocean rolling between us, that I was never to see again. My relations believed that I was living in America; they knew nothing of this expedition, or that I had joined it, and they would probably never hear of it. None of them would ever hear of my end, and so best, I thought, since it is to be like this. They would often wonder why I never wrote to them, or why I did not come back, and they would be expecting me years after I was dead and dust. And M——, my pretty brown-eyed cousin that loved me so well. Was this to be the end of all my promises?

When I said good-bye to her on leaving home, my heart felt as if it would burst, although the separation was only to be for a few years. My mother looked on, and never suspected that there was anything between us; I bore up so well until I was out of sight. It was only six months since then, yet it seemed a long time, for I had lived long since then. Every scene or incident in which we had ever been associated, crowded my memory on that night. The rambles that we had often taken together along the banks of the river, or on the sea-shore, in the far-away old country. Or when we went in the long summer days to see some old castle or ruined abbey, and I used to help her to climb the walls, and ask her to sing for me, as we sat there and looked out over the country; and sometimes a passer-by would stop and listen to music such as he had never heard before—that glorious voice that even the angels might envy! And when we visited some "Holy Well," and drank the water out of wooden bowls, and looked in amazement at the crutches and rags—mementoes left by grateful invalids—that hung from the trees that grew round the spring, how we listened to the stories, told by the simple old country women, of the cures of the blind and the lame brought about by drinking the waters, and praying to the patron saint of the well. I recollected that at a house where we visited, there hung on the wall of one of the rooms a picture of a dead man, with the moon and stars shining on him, and by his side there knelt an angel, or a woman, and underneath there was a legend that M—— read aloud, and which I have never forgotten. There are some lines, whether of poetry or declamation, which, when once heard, somehow cling to our memories, and we find ourselves repeating them years afterwards. I seemed to hear my cousin's voice once more—that voice that would never again fill my ears or thrill my heart with joy—reading aloud:

> The sun shall be no more thy light by day,
> Neither for brightness shall the moon give light unto thee;
> But the Lord shall be unto thee an everlasting light,
> And thy God thy glory.

"Has the sun then set for me for ever?" I asked myself. "Shall I nevermore see the sun rise, or meet my companions? Will I be shot as a spy or a criminal?" No; I would preserve my independence to the end, and die a free man; no executioner should perform his ghastly office on me.

I had my revolver on me, and I drew and cocked

it, and felt if the percussion caps were on the nipples, for there were no breech-loaders then. My tears were falling fast, I admit that weakness; but vanity at last came to my relief, and even out there alone, with no one to see me, I felt ashamed of my tears, and thought: what?—a soldier crying because he has to die? Psha! What would my companions say if they knew it, or what would M—— think if she could see me? It is but a moment's torture, and all is over. But when we are young and in robust health, we think it hard to die, and cling to life as long as we can. At last I succeeded in suppressing my emotions, and wiped the tears from my eyes with the sleeve of my shirt. I got over the bitter pang, and resigned myself calmly to my fate.

Just then a thought shot through me: why not shout defiance at the enemy? They would then fire on me, or try and capture me, and if they failed to kill me I could still do it myself before they could lay hands on me. But they might only wound me, and after all take me alive. No, I must make sure. I grasped my pistol with both hands, and crossed my thumbs on the trigger. I put the barrel in my mouth, and I was on the point of completing the final act, when a flame burst out in front of me. I hesitated. Hope began to dawn once more. I lowered my hand, and carefully uncocked the revolver, and replaced it in my belt; and as I did so, another fire broke out into flame, and from the smoke beyond the fires I could see where other fires were smothered with green branches and grass, so as to create a smoke to drive away the mosquitoes.

What a change had come over me in a few moments, or as Scott writes:

"How diverse and opposite within the space of a few moments are the emotions of a human soul! How sudden are its changes from apprehension to self-complacency, and how in a flash its outlook on existence alters from dark to light?"

Before me, with the light of the fire shining on it, not twenty yards from where I sat, I saw a bunch of bananas, and I crawled eagerly forward, and soon had them in my possession; and I had no sooner done so when my eyes fell on another and a better bunch on another plant, but somewhat near to where a Spanish sentry was pacing backwards and forwards. But I was determined to have them, and leaving those that I had already cut down near the tree, I crept along on my hands and knees, only moving when the sentry turned to walk away from me. I reached them and cut them down, but in doing so, made a slight rustling noise with the large leaves, which I could not well avoid. The sentry heard me, and halted in his walk, and wheeling round, brought his musket to "prime," and challenged.

I was lying partly on my back where I had slipped and fallen. I lay perfectly immovable, with the bunch of bananas at my side. The sentry appeared to be looking me straight in the face and listening. He was undecided, and I, thinking that probably he could see my eyes, as we sometimes see the eyes of a wild animal when light shines on them in a dark place, almost closed them, only lifting the lids sufficiently to get a glimpse of his movements.

Will he fire, I thought? Does he see me?

It was with a feeling of relief that I saw him recover his musket after looking towards me for some time, and slowly pace away from me, as if he had decided that he was mistaken; but he did not take many steps before he turned again, and stood still for a while in a listening attitude.

I remained immovable all the while. He walked a little way towards me, and looked intently again in my direction; but at last, as if satisfied, he turned on his beat and walked away from me. He was suspicious, and that troubled me, so when he turned his back, I drew my revolver and cocked it, and I drew up my bunch of bananas in front of my body as a kind of screen, and I determined to be beforehand with him, should he show any suspicions of my presence again. Every time that he returned from the end of his walk, he looked hard in my direction, and I did not attempt to move until I observed that he appeared to be reassured; and then, whenever he turned his back, I moved away a few yards, but always keeping my face to him, and always remaining perfectly still before he turned round to walk in my direction, and keeping so until he turned his back on me again.

In this manner I was gradually increasing the distance between us, when I recollected that I had another bunch of bananas to pick up—the first that I had cut down—and I had to make a side movement to reach it. This I accomplished successfully, and was beginning to move off again, when all the fires went out suddenly, and all was darkness once more. I only moved away sufficiently to be out of sight of the sentry, if the fires should blaze up again, and I stood up and looked all round. I looked in the direction in which I thought our camp lay in the village, but nothing was to be seen, no light anywhere, and there was nothing for it but to wait patiently. I did not know where I was, only that I was near the enemy's sentries—perhaps in their rear. I had got what I had come out for, after a good deal of fatigue and some hairbreadth escapes, from my own hands as well as from the enemy's, and I was determined to get back safely with my bananas if possible. So I sat down to wait for the fires to blaze up again to guide me. In the meantime, as I felt hungry, I felt the bananas all over for the ripest, and ate a good meal of them, and strange to say, there, close to the enemy, I dropped off to sleep.

How long I slept I cannot tell, but I might have slept until the morning if it had not been for the mosquitoes. When I looked about me there were some fires smouldering in the enemy's camp, some of them not more than a hundred yards from me.

I got up, and began to drag my two bunches of bananas away with me, I knew not where; but I wanted to get as far away from the enemy as possible, while I had the light of their fires to guide me. I moved away without interruption, until I found that I was sinking the fires—that is, they were disappearing from me.

I was getting into low ground; but where? Was I in the enemy's rear? Had I got the whole Spanish force between me and my friends? I was fatigued and heated with dragging the heavy bunches of bananas after me, and now what was I to do? I knew that I must be some distance from the Spanish camp; but in which direction?

From the distance I had walked since I woke up, I ought to have reached San Jacinto long before, if I had gone in that direction.

I cursed Ashton for not keeping a fire burning, and I thought of the wind again; but I should have thought of that when I first started to go back after escaping the sentry. I found out how the wind was blowing, although it was barely perceptible, and I reasoned this way. If I am in the enemy's rear, and I walk with my face to the wind, it will lead me right on to him, and I shall be able to see his fires in time to check myself and alter my course; and if I am not in his rear, the wind will lead me away from him, and that will do for the present, or until daylight. So after a short rest, I started again, and walked some distance, when I struck on a little brook, and thinking it might be the one that ran by the village, I put my hand in the water to find out which way the stream was running, and having ascertained that, I now had to determine whether San Jacinto was up-stream or down-stream. I decided to go down-stream, and I had not gone far before I came to a place that I recognised where we used to take water, where the stream ran close to the village, and I soon got in sight of the ditch, and moved cautiously along parallel to it, so as to get round to where I had started from.

Whilst moving along, a voice hailed me in a loud whisper:

"Is that you?"

"Yes," I answered, for it was Ashton who called.

"Oh, where have you been all night? I was beginning to give you up as lost. Have you got anything?"

"Yes."

"Let me carry one bunch for you."

"Here, you can carry both, for I am tired out," and I turned both bunches of bananas over to him and followed him, and we were soon safe inside the ditch, without any one else being the wiser.

I had been wandering about nearly all night, for it was near daylight when I got back. Ashton heard the shot of the Spanish sentry, and when I did not return after a reasonable time, he concluded that I was struck, and either killed or wounded. He knew that I would do all in my power to crawl back to the ditch, if I was not dead or badly wounded; and he wandered about all through the night, in a line parallel with the ditch, calling every now and again, in a voice below his breath: "Are you there?" until at last he found me. Good, honest, kind-hearted Ashton! unselfish to a degree rarely to be met with. He would have shared his shirt or his last mouthful with me, and would not have hesitated to risk his life to do me a service.

CHAPTER XV.

Enemy reinforced with artillery--They open fire—Shells bursting in the *plaza*—Death of Hodson—The night march — Overtaken by the enemy—Defeated — Escape wounded—My horse saves me—Captain Ryan wounded—Death of Storey.

THE next morning there was a movement in the Spanish camp. They had received reinforcements, and a battery of six howitzers had arrived, and they were not long in letting us know it. They opened fire on us with the howitzers at about five hundred yards, and soon began to send their shell into the *plaza*; but they had chosen their distance too close, for with our Minié rifles we dropped many of their gunners, and they were obliged to limber up and take new ground a couple of hundred yards further to the rear, when they again opened on us, and kept at it all day.

Our position was beginning to get untenable, and every one could see that things could not go on much longer as they were. The enemy kept up their fire unceasingly .until dark night, compelling us to keep under cover wherever we could, and as best we could, to avoid the bursting shells that were playing sad havoc with the horses, for they were loose in the *plaza*. One shell went through the roof of a house where some of our sick lay, and bursting inside, killed many of them. We expected that when the enemy ceased firing, they would immediately assault the place, and try to take it, and we stood to arms all night in expectation of the attack; but the night passed quietly without any attempt being made, and at dawn of day they opened fire again, and we saw that we were in for another day's bombardment before the assault would be made; or perhaps they intended to shell us out.

It was well for us that the enemy did not use percussion fuses in their shells, they were fitted with time fuses, and when they struck and buried themselves in the sand and earth, they often got choked, and the shells did not burst; still, as things were, we could not stand it much longer. A good many of our horses were killed, and if we did not march out soon we would have to go on foot.

That evening, as soon as the enemy ceased firing, we were hurriedly mustered in the *plaza*, and prepared to evacuate the place. Our commander told us that we could not expect to pass another day without being assailed by the enemy, who would in all probability have assaulted the place before, if they had known how weak we were; and as there was no likelihood of our being able to reach the mountains, or to join our friends in our present weak condition, and surrounded as we were by the numerous and well-armed forces of the enemy, he thought it his duty to assemble us, and explain clearly our position and prospects, and hear what we had to say on the matter. If we decided to remain any longer in this place, we must make up our minds to die within the next twenty-four hours, or forty-eight hours at the furthest. If we marched out that night, which we could easily do, as the enemy had no guard near the watering-place in the brook, we might be able to put a good many miles between us and the village before they discovered that we had evacuated it; and by marching for the river Canto, and coasting down towards the sea, we would be likely to fall in with a schooner or coasting vessel, for the river was navigable for small craft for fifty or sixty miles from its mouth, and small vessels often came up that distance to load. If we succeeded in capturing one of these vessels, we could drop down to the mouth of the river, and make sail for the English island of Jamaica, not more than a day's sail distant with a good breeze.

Every one agreed to this proposal at once without demur, and we immediately went to catch and saddle the horses. There were still enough to mount every man in the place, but the *very* sick had to be left behind to the tender mercies of the enemy; there was no remedy for it. If they were to shoot them, it would only shorten their sufferings, for a few days were the most that some of them could expect to live, they were so far gone, and the Spaniards might not think it worth their while to shoot them.

All the spare arms and ammunition were buried under the floor of one of the houses. Food—such as we had—and water, was placed within reach of the sick, and we were about to march out, when another painful incident occurred. Major Hodson, who had been sick for a long time, discovered that he was too weak and far gone to sit a horse, and knowing the alternative, he cut his throat, rather than be left behind alive. He was seen at the last moment, and delayed us a little while longer. We dug a grave for him in the *plaza*, outside the church door, and after burying him, we filed quietly down to the stream, crossed it, and rode up the opposite bank without meeting any obstruction until we came to the trees, where we halted for a few minutes to see if all was well, and to make sure of the few villagers, whom we compelled to go with us for some distance, for fear that they might inform the enemy of our movements, to gain favour for themselves. We wheeled to the left, and skirted the timber in our march. The villagers were told that they were wanted to guide us round the village to the rear of the enemy's encampment, and show us the best road to the mountains, and we gave them to understand that we brought all of them with us, to prevent them from informing the enemy. There were not forty altogether, and most of them were women. We strongly suspected that they would run to the Spaniards with the news of the evacuation as soon as they were free, or if they did not go voluntarily, the enemy would compel them to disclose the direction we had taken, and the march round to the rear of the enemy's encampment was merely a ruse to deceive them as well as the enemy.

When we reached the place aimed at, the Sanjacinteros, or people from the village, were dismissed with profuse thanks, and we continued our march towards the mountains for a short distance, until those people were well on their way back, when we wheeled to the right, and altered our line of march. Daylight came, and we still held on our way, without stay or halt, until about midday, when a halt was called for a few minutes; but it began to rain, and we moved on again, and jogged along in the rain all the afternoon on our jaded horses. To our surprise, the Spaniards came upon us at sundown, and we had scarcely time to fall into any kind of order to receive them. We immediately dismounted, and sent the horses, with the sick men who were not able to fight, to the rear amongst some trees, whilst we fronted to receive the attack of the enemy.

They came on fiercely enough, and although our fire was good and well delivered, it did not check them; but they suffered severely while they were in the open. We were well protected by the wood, on the edge of which we had taken up our position; but they had got into the wood on our flanks, and as the night closed in their fire seemed almost to surround us. They lapped over our flanks, and we had to fall back repeatedly, to avoid being completely surrounded.

Our commander, Ryan, seemed to be everywhere, cheering and encouraging the men. He appeared to be exposing himself needlessly, and seemed to bear a charmed life, for no shot struck him, although he was always where the fire was hottest, and men were dropping fast round him.

I have since then often thought that he did not wish to survive the disaster. He must have known that there was not the slightest chance for us. To surrender would have been death in any case, and an ignominious death that he would not submit to, and he knew that most, if not all the men, were of the same way of thinking; for after all, when one has to die, it is easier to die fighting, when one's blood is up, than to be led out like a lamb to the slaughter.

The Spaniards pushed us steadily back until they had driven us through the piece of open timber to the more open ground beyond it, where they could better see our reduced numbers, although it was now night; when, as if ashamed of being held in check so long by such an inferior enemy, they charged us with shouts of "Viva España!" and completely overwhelmed us.

All was now confusion and massacre. It was all over with us now; every man for himself. In the rush I was knocked down, and surrounded by the enemy; but I managed to regain my feet again, and using my rifle as a shillelagh, in Donnybrook Fair fashion, swinging it with both hands, I battered my way out of the mêlée, but I was knocked down again in my efforts to reach the horses, but I finally succeeded. Everything seemed lost. The few that were left alive of our men were scattered about in twos and threes, and surrounded by groups of the enemy. A little knot of them had succeeded in reaching the horses about the same time that I did, and were mounting; but the enemy's horsemen were now on the ground, and seeing what we were at, they rushed at us, and in a moment we were again surrounded.

I was mounted on what in Spanish is called a *rosilla*, or red roan horse. He was tall for a Cuban horse, but had never been properly broken in, and was a vicious brute, and I had to be constantly on my guard for him, for he would try and kick at anybody who went to saddle him up—not because he was sore or galled on the back, for some horses that are otherwise quiet enough, will kick when the girths are tightened, if their backs are anyway sore. My roan was perfectly sound on the back; but he was a vicious brute, and quick to mount, for when he felt one tighten up the reins and catch the stirrup-leather preparatory to mounting, he did not give one time to put his foot in the iron, but immediately bounded forward, and I had to be very smart in jumping on his back. He could not well play that trick where he was crowded in amongst other horses, and surrounded that night; but he kicked at everything that came near his heels. When saddled and mounted, if his rider, in turning round in his seat to look behind, or to speak to any one, rested his hand on his croup, he immediately began to buck-jump, and strike out with his heels behind; and this vice of his stood me in good stead that night, for two of the enemy's horsemen closing on my rear, came very close to the roan's heels, and as I turned in the saddle to show face to them, I rested my sword-hand heavily on his hips, when he immediately started jumping and kicking. One of the Spaniards made a prod with his sabre at him, but he only just caught the point of it, as he had kicked an open space about his heels; and one of our fellows took advantage of it to make his escape out of the crowd, and darted past me, and I seeing this, wheeled round and quickly followed him, barely escaping a sweeping blow from the sabre of one of the Spaniards, by bending down on the horse's neck as I flew past; but I lost my hat, for the sabre caught the leaf of it, and carried it off my head.

We rode for some timber a little way ahead, and right before us was one of our sick men sitting quietly on his horse, and holding a led horse, with two ammunition boxes strapped to the pack-saddle. It was so dark that I did not recognise him until I got alongside, and shouted to him to escape, at the same time striking his horses with the flat of my sword, so as to start them off in a gallop, when I discovered him to be poor little Jos Storey.

"Ah!" he said, "let me be, sergeant; I can't gallop, I'm played out. What matter if they kill me? I'm dying, anyway."

I said some words of encouragement to him,.

and drove him on with me. We rode straight for the trees, expecting rest and shelter there, for our horses were tired with the march all that day and the night before, and could not carry us far, and if we had been pursued we could have been easily overtaken. Luckily, we were not followed. Probably the enemy's horses were in no better condition than ours, for they must have ridden hard to have caught up on us.

It was night when we got away, and completely dark long before we reached the friendly shelter of the timber, where we drew rein and dismounted, and led our horses in amongst the trees. Poor little Storey had to be lifted off his horse, and carried into the wood, and placed on the ground with his back against a tree. My other companion was an older soldier, and belonged to Wingate's company; but he knew no more than I did as to the fate of the others. I supposed that they had all been destroyed or taken prisoners; but he thought that some of them had escaped in another direction.

After a while he said to me:

"Hadn't we better see if there are any of our fellows hiding about here?"

"Yes," I replied; "but how will you do it?"

"We'll whistle to them," said he.

We went to the edge of the wood, and sitting

down, my companion began to whistle a bar or two of a popular air, in a low key at first, and after a while, louder; but we got no response. He then went out in the open, and further down to the left, while I remained where I was, so that I could direct him to where Storey and the horses lay. He whistled "Yankee Doodle," when some one called in English: "Who's there?" He answered: "Wingate's." When the other replied: "We're Ryan's. How many are ye?"

"Only three."

"We're eight," said the others; but neither of the officers whose names were mentioned were with them, the men made use of their names to designate the company they belonged to.

When they came up to where I was waiting, I got into conversation with some of them, and discovered that they had made their escape rather earlier than what we did, and could give us no information. Most of them were wounded, and lay down on the ground to rest themselves, while the others were talking. While lying stretched out on the ground, one of them noticed the loom of a man on foot, and leading a horse after him by the bridle, a little way over from where we stood. I thought it was one of the enemy, and challenged him in Spanish, ordering him to halt. It turned out to be Ryan, alone and wounded. He had three wounds, a gun-shot wound and two sabre cuts, one of which was on the side of his head, and had left a piece of the scalp and one of his ears hanging down on his neck. We bound up his wounds roughly, and were afterwards joined by some more of the men, making in all twenty-seven or twenty-eight men, and that was all that was left of our force, and many of them were wounded.

We waited here, by the direction of our officer, and signalled for nearly two hours, but as no more joined us, we concluded that there were no more; and as it would be dangerous to wait any longer in this neighbourhood, for the enemy were near, and would be searching the country round for us in the morning, we prepared to march. One of the men said that he had seen Captain Wingate and some others get clear away, but in a different direction to the one taken by us.

There were three Cubans amongst the men who had joined us, good fellows who behaved well at all times, and stood by us to the last, and to whom, perhaps, we owed our escape in the end, as they acted as guides, to a certain extent. They now took the lead, and we marched through the wood on foot, in single file, and leading our horses; but we had not advanced a quarter of a mile before we had to cut a pathway through the tangled undergrowth. Some of the strongest men went forward and opened a way with the sword, and as my company was the only one armed with swords, the men belonging to it who escaped were in front, the sick and wounded in the middle, and a few sound men in the rear. Only one man went ahead at a time, and he only cut a sufficient opening for himself and horse to pass; as he got tired he fell back, and another took his place. I had no rifle, for I threw mine away when I came out of the fight, as the stock was broken and rendered useless from the treatment I gave it in thrashing my way to my horse. I was in front when we started, with one of the Cubans; but Ryan sent me to the rear, with orders to have the pathway concealed or covered in again behind us, so that the enemy would not be able to see that we had entered the dense part of the wood. This I did with the assistance of a Cuban and my friend Ashton, who was one of the few who escaped with a whole skin.

Ryan was in the middle of the file with a Cuban, who, with a light and a compass, directed the men on the march; but it was very difficult to keep anything like a straight line. This was only a narrow belt of wood, for we soon got through it, and emerged on an open savanna, which we crossed without halting, to another thick wood on the further side, where we halted on the edge of the forest, as there was good grass there, and we unbitted the horses, and loosened the girths, and held them by the halters and bridles while they fed. We had been scarcely an hour here, when the sky began to brighten in the east, the sign of the coming day, and I passed the order to "girth up" and march, and we again entered the wood in single file as before, cutting our way with our swords, and covering up our tracks behind us; but we soon had daylight to assist us in making our way.

Now and again in our march through the forest, we came upon small open spaces where there was a hollow, or depression in the ground, and sometimes a pool of stagnant water, and as a matter of course, swarms of mosquitoes; or where a decayed tree or two had fallen, dragging down others of smaller size with it; or where the trees were riven and blackened by lightning and storm. We halted at one of these openings at noon, and rested for two or three hours, and I had time and light to examine my leg. In the early part of the night before, when we got away from the enemy, I felt that I was wounded in one of my legs, for the rags which I had wrapped round it, and that served for shoe, stocking, and gaiter, were soaking wet, and as it felt too warm for perspiration, I knew that it must be blood; but as it did not inconvenience me at the time, I judged that it could not be serious. I now felt my leg stiff and painful, and I had to loosen the fastenings of my leg-gear to ease the pain.

I must explain here that our shoes were worn out, and we went with our feet and legs wrapped round with any pieces of cloth or rags that we could lay our hands on, and fastened with strips of horse or mule's skin—pretty much in the fashion that Italian shepherd-boys are represented in pictures. I don't know if the shepherd-boys take off their leg-gear every night, but our boys scarcely took theirs off once a week. From this statement the reader can imagine the condition of our feet, after tramping, oftentimes, through mud and water, and anon in a hot sun, that quickly baked the mud on our legs.

I found a wound in my right leg in front about an inch and a quarter long. It had been inflicted with a blunt weapon, and I had also, strange to say, a black eye; but I have not the slightest recollection of how I came by either. We had no doctor with us now—our German surgeon, poor fellow, was among the killed or missing—and my friend Ashton acted the part of *médico* for me.

After siesta we marched again, cutting our pathway as before; but we did not consider it necessary to cover over our track any longer. My leg was painful all that afternoon, and I was glad when night came, although night found us still in the forest; but our Cubans told us that we would be clear of it early next day. We were very hungry, for we had had nothing to eat since we left San Jacinto. However, we were cheered by the thought of getting through next day, and reaching a friendly plantation, where we might hope to find something eatable, and be able to recruit our strength, and attend to our wounded; so we rested all night in the wood.

In the night some one called me up, telling me that Storey thought that he was dying, and had been calling for me for some time. I was very sleepy and tired, but I got up and moved over near him, and lay down on the ground by his side, and taking one of his hands in mine, I asked him what he wanted me for. The poor little fellow said:

"Sergeant, I guess I'm played out—I'm dying."

"Nonsense," I said, "you will be all right to-morrow. We expect to reach a plantation early to-morrow, where there is an abundance of everything and a good doctor; he'll soon put you on your legs again. Now go to sleep."

"I hear you are wounded; is that so?"

"Nothing to speak of, Storey," I replied; "but go to sleep—I am very tired and can't keep awake. We'll speak about it in the morning; there's a good fellow. I'll do anything you want me to do in the morning."

"No, sergeant, I won't keep you long; I know you're tired and wounded—if you'll only mind the address, can you write it down?"

"No, Storey, what are you talking about? You're dreaming—what address? I have no pencil or paper. Where would I get them? And how could I write in the dark? Tell me what you want, Storey. I won't forget in. Come, there's a good fellow." And as he did not speak, I said brusquely: "D——n it, man, be quick, and don't keep me all night."

"Don't get vexed—sergeant—I'll—be through— in a moment—give me—a little time—I can't— speak fast—listen—If ever—you get back—to the States——"

"Yes, Storey, go on."

"Or anywhere—away from here."

"Yes, all right, go on."

"I want you—to write—to my mother."

"Aw—right."

"My mother—her address is."

"Aw—right, I know."

"Are you—awake—sergeant?"

"Ye—a—s—go—on."

"Mrs. M. Storey—are you listening?"

"Uhm."

"Thirty —, —— Street, Boston—Boston."

I recollected no more. I had dropped off asleep

while he was speaking to me. Boston was the last word—the last sound that I heard from his lips.

When Ashton woke me in the morning I was lying beside Storey, on my face, with his hand still in mine, as I had taken it when I lay down at his side; but it was cold enough now. I started up in horror to find that I had been sleeping with a corpse. The poor lad must have died talking to me, while I lay fast asleep at his side. His eyes and mouth were wide open, and there he lay stark, and staring up at the sky.

Oh, how horribly callous and selfish suffering and misery can make us! How pained I was to think that I had spoken harshly to the poor lad in his last moments! The remorse of knowing that, through my selfishness—for want of a little self-denial —I had neglected to listen to the poor dying boy's last words, or to hear his last message to his mother! She would mourn him lost and dead, probably. Perhaps he ran away from home, like many other boys, and she may not have known where he was. She would never know now what had become of him, or that he died peacefully and quietly, and was not mangled in bloody strife like many of his companions.

I felt so keenly the necessity of some atonement for my want of feeling or want of thought the night before, that I would not allow any one to touch him, and I performed the last offices for my dead comrade with my own hands. With our swords and our hands Ashton and I scooped out a grave for him, and I carried him in my arms and laid him in it rolled up in his blanket. He was not heavy to carry, poor boy! for he had wasted away until there was scarcely anything left but skin and bone. We covered him in with earth, and placed a rustic wooden cross at his head, and left him.

While Ashton and I were engaged burying Storey the others had started on the march, and tired and hungry we joined them, and took our turn in cutting through the jungle. Many of the men were stiff and worn out, and scarcely able to move, much less work, and we saw no alligator pears, or anything eatable in this forest. At last, some time after midday, we emerged from this wood, and were gratified at seeing signs of cultivation before us, and some distance out in the clearing appeared the establishment of the friendly planter.

CHAPTER XVI.

A friendly planter—Curing the sick—Shift our quarters—Rest—I get well—Men get lock-jaw—On the march again—A thunderstorm—The "Isla"—Safety.

WE were well received by the planter, who told us that his house, and everything he had, was at our disposal, but he was anxious at the same time that we should make as short a stay as possible at or near his place; and we told him that forty-eight hours' rest would recruit ourselves and our horses, after which we would leave him; we wished, also, to make inquiries as to the whereabouts of the enemy, their movements and scouting parties, so that we could avoid them.

The first night at the plantation we feasted and slept well, but now that our immediate wants were supplied and we had time to rest and think, the thought of little Storey and my remissness would recur to me and weigh heavily on me. I was not satisfied with myself and the part that I had played towards him. If it had been any one else, if it had been Ashton that he had called instead of me, to confide to him his dying request, I felt sure that he would have behaved better.

The only excuse, the only palliation for my behaviour was that I was but a boy of seventeen—younger even than Storey—and had not slept since we marched out of San Jacinto, two days and two nights. As my commander was wounded, I, being the only sergeant among the survivors, was in charge of the men, and I did not have time to close my eyes during the two or three short halts that were made on the march; besides, I really did not think that he was so near death.

Our sick and wounded, who were more than half our number, were well attended to here at this plantation, or *hacienda*, as it was called; but now that we had time to look round and consider our condition, it was easy to be seen that it would take a good many "forty-eight hours" before we would be in a fit condition to move again.

The planter, good fellow as he was, got uneasy on seeing this, and no wonder, for it would be death to him as well as to us if the enemy found us at his place. We compromised matters by arranging to move to a secure place in the woods, and distant about two miles from the establishment. The planter agreed to supply all our wants as regards food, and we shifted our camp, but we kept a guard at his house to make sure of things. He gave us an ointment to cure our wounds, but as his whole stock would not go very far amongst us, he supplied us with the ingredients for making it, and we found it very effective in most cases. It is, I believe, an old Spanish remedy, and the recipe is: One part of turpentine and four of beeswax are melted together in an earthenware pot over a slow fire, and one-eighth part of powdered alum and one-ninth part of powdered camphor are added, the whole to be stirred rapidly until it forms a perfectly homogeneous mass. When used it has to be melted and dropped on the wound, which is then covered up, and this has to be renewed every two or three days until it heals up. Ryan had a gun-shot wound on the left arm, but this soon got better, as the ball had passed clean through the fleshy part of the arm without injuring the bone. The sabre cuts on the shoulder and head gave most trouble.

Some of the sick and wounded men got rapidly better, and others got rapidly worse, although the treatment of all was alike. Ryan sent for me on the second day of our arrival here, and told me to caution the men not to tell any one about the plantation that we suspected that Comandante

Fernandez had been killed, as the Señora, or wife of the *Haciendero*, was a near relation of his. This lady behaved very kindly to us, giving us all the linen and rags that she had for our sores, and we had an abundance of fruit of all kinds while we remained here, but there was a great scarcity of meat. There was, however, no scarcity of snakes and vermin of all kinds, for the first day we took possession of our new encampment in the forest we killed over a dozen of all sizes, and the men amused themselves and passed their time in skinning the largest, and covering their belts with the skins. I observed that, even when divested of their heads, and their hides, some of these snakes still wriggled about on the ground. The Cubans told us that they would not die until night—even when cut into pieces.

Venomous reptiles and annoying insects abounded here; centipedes and scorpions, ants and mosquitoes irritated and tormented us night and day. No breeze, not even a gale of wind, could reach the encampment; it was so closely shut in and surrounded with the dense undergrowth, that all the men who could crawl, or get assistance from their comrades, passed the day, and often the night, on the edge of the clearing; and even there it was not much better, unless a breeze happened to be blowing.

We could not enjoy the coolness of the shade

for the flies and the mosquitoes; and our strength was exhausted, and our lives wearied out in the constant endeavour to ward off their attacks. Fortunately for me I was one of those whose wounds healed quickly, for now that I could rest my leg, and dress the wound and keep it clean, it soon healed up, and a week after our arrival I was able to go anywhere, with the aid of a crutch, and enjoy myself.

It may seem strange for a young man wounded, and obliged to use a crutch, and attend on companions sick and wounded, and with all the disagreeable circumstances enumerated, to talk of enjoyment. Yet, notwithstanding all its drawbacks, I enjoyed life there as I have rarely enjoyed it anywhere else. The freedom, for the time, from all control, from the anxiety and fatigue of the battle and the march, and the continual alertness which had never ceased for a moment, night or day, since the night we landed on the coast, this to me was happiness, and I suppose to the others who had health; to any one else it would, doubtless, be misery enough, but as happiness is comparative, one would have to pass through the same experiences that we did to be able to appreciate it.

Discipline was relaxed here; indeed there was no necessity for it, we were so few, nor any one to enforce it. Our commander lay sick and wounded in a hammock given him by the planter, and the time of the sound men was taken up in nursing their sick comrades. We made little shelter huts for them and for ourselves, open at the sides, to keep off the rain and the dew, for we suffered as much from the climate, I dare say, as from anything else; from the heat and the moisture. The air was heavy and saturated with miasma, which tells hard on the white man, added to which was the plague of being constantly surrounded by noxious vermin and venomous insects that preyed on our bodies, and rendered sleep or rest difficult; nevertheless, with all these annoyances to contend against, Nature would assert herself, and when overcome with weariness we could sleep, and habit at last made stoics of us, and we became reconciled to every discomfort.

Wounds are difficult to heal in the tropics, and some of the men got lock-jaw and died; some from very simple wounds. Luckily our commander got better. The lady of the *hacienda* was very kind to him, and nearly every day she sent him some dainty or present, which was turned over to the men, for Ryan scarcely touched any food while he lay unwell. As soon as he was able to go about he became more exacting in matters of discipline, and the men were obliged to be more orderly. There were stated times for everything, and though few in number, we soon fell back into the old routine of mounting guard and posting sentries, although we only mustered nineteen men altogether.

The place where we were encamped was not healthy, and as soon as Ryan was sufficiently recovered to move about, he determined to move away from it, and he wished to select a more healthy spot to convalesce in; besides, there was the probability of our whereabouts becoming known to the Spanish scouting parties that were now scouring the country, for we had been three weeks in the one place, and all the people about the plantation, black and white, were well aware of our character, and that we were in arms against the Government. Their master and employer was friendly, but he could not guarantee the fidelity of every one about him. We had also learned that the Canto, our objective point, and the only navigable river on the south coast of Cuba, was closely watched by the Spaniards. The coast was guarded by their war vessels and gunboats, and all the creeks and small streams were patrolled by guard boats, and our chances of escaping in that direction were very slight.

As there was no longer any motive for remaining in this neighbourhood, or striving to reach the Canto, it was decided that we should march west until we reached a part of the island that had taken no active part as yet in the insurrection, and where there were few or no troops, and where we might travel with less risk and reach the coast. Once there we would have to trust to chance and some friendly vessel to get away. Or perhaps Ryan had still hope of being able to join some Cuban force, or of falling in with some other American expedition that had landed on the coast; but we had to get well first. Many of the men could barely sit on horseback, and we had to find a healthier encampment than the one we were in.

An old negro, who had been brought up by the *Haciendero's* father, and whose fidelity he assured us of, was sent to guide us to a secure resting-place. It was a long way off, we were told, several days' march to the westward in the direction in which we wished to go; but we could travel slowly —in fact, we could not travel any other way but slowly—and it would be better than remaining here. We started on our journey on a foggy morning, and after crossing an open savanna, we entered the wood by a forest road or track, known to our guide, from which we emerged from time to time on open glades, where we could obtain occasionally a good view of the surrounding country; but we did not see a single habitation on our march. Whether it was that our guide purposely avoided them, or that there were none to see, we knew not.

After the usual siesta, or midday rest, we continued our march, at times across short stretches of open savanna, and again through forest, our guide always choosing the highest ground in the forest, as the wood was more open there, and freer from undergrowth; for there are no roads in the interior of Cuba, but what the traveller makes for himself with his axe and *machéte*, and if they are not frequented, they soon get completely obliterated by the rank tropical vegetation. At night we lit fires, as there was no restriction, and cooked and ate our supper in freedom—except from mosquitoes—after which we lay down until morning, and with the first streak of day we were again in the saddle and on the march.

Our marching was all done by daylight—no more night work—but we made slow progress, for we had to regulate our rate of marching to the strength of the weakest man, and it was more like a funeral procession than anything else. Our guide took us by the most unfrequented route, or else the country through which we passed was uninhabited, for we only met one individual in our march, and he looked frightened at seeing us.

On the evening of the fifth day we encamped for the night on the border of another dense forest; we had spent all day in crossing an extensive savanna, and had the good fortune to shoot three deer, and as we found some alligator pears growing wild in the forest, we enjoyed a good supper, and passed the best night of any since we left San Jacinto.

The alligator pear was plentiful in this place, and although I never liked it, and never touched it if I could get anything else, yet the men seemed to like it, and I was often glad to get it when hunger pressed me. It is a soft, pulpy, insipid kind of fruit, in outside appearance not unlike a large English pear spotted over with red; there is a stone in the centre of it, and when the fruit is ripe and fit for use the stone becomes loose inside, and can be shaken about.

In the morning the old negro, after vainly searching about for an opening in the forest, told us that we would have to cut a road to reach our proposed new encampment; but before starting to work we hurried our preparations for breakfast, as the sky was getting overcast, and we could hear the rumbling of an approaching thunderstorm.

We had scarcely finished our meal when night seemed to have closed in on us once more, it grew so dark, and an impending sense of fear seemed to take possession of both men and horses, as if something awful was about to happen. Everything was hushed and quiet. The men scarcely spoke to each other, and when they did so it was in whispers. All at once, without a moment's warning, the storm burst on us—a veritable West Indian tornado—a fierce blast that swept everything before it, scattering the embers of our fires through the forest, and twisting and wrenching off the branches of the trees around us. This was followed by flashes of lightning and incessant peals of thunder, and although we were accustomed to thunder and lightning, for scarcely a week passed since our landing without rain and thunder, for it was the rainy season in the West Indies, we had never experienced anything like this. It was grand, no doubt, but terribly appalling. Flash succeeded flash unceasingly, the deafening crashes of the thunder following each flash of lightning in quick succession. The ground fairly shook, as if about to open up and swallow us, and the whole forest was lit up with the lightning. Large trees were every moment splitting from top to root and flying in pieces as if a mine had been exploded in the heart of each. The horses came in amongst the men as if they sought their protection, and cowered and crouched almost to the ground with fear. The rain poured down in sheets, and this pandemonium lasted for about half an hour, when it gradually subsided.

In all my subsequent experience in other parts of the world I can scarcely recall one other *tor-*

menta to equal that West Indian one; and speaking for myself, it was with a feeling of relief I saw it subside without harming any one, for while it lasted I certainly had as lively a sense of fear as ever I felt in facing the enemy—perhaps more so, for no matter what military or other writers say to the contrary, I feel confident that every civilised man has a sense of fear when he is called on to face death. It is part of our nature, and we cannot get rid of it. Some men with a stronger will are able to dominate the feeling, and show less of it than others, or suppress it altogether; but it is there nevertheless, and the soldier and the sailor has to keep it under.

The believer in Christianity is doubtful if he is prepared to appear before his Maker, while the atheist hesitates at the thought of utter annihilation.

The writers who relate anecdotes of celebrated men, soldiers and sailors, can surely know very little of human nature when they tell us, as I once read, of Nelson, when a boy, asking the meaning of the word *fear*. "He could not be made to understand it! He never knew it!" At least, so we are told.

Another writer, an American, tells us that General Grant, when a boy at school, came across the word *can't*, and did not know the meaning of it, and could not understand it. All this is silly nonsense, and no one knows it better than the truly brave man; and at the risk of being considered presumptuous, I will say that the man who never knew fear never performed a gallant action.

When the storm cleared away we wrung the water out of our clothes and began to work to open a pathway through the wood, to what the old negro called the " Isla," and after half a day's work we debouched from the forest on to it. The "Isla" we found to be an open space of ground of about from five to six hundred acres in extent, and of an irregular form, and surrounded with an impenetrable forest, or nearly so, for on our left hand, close to where we came in, there were about a hundred yards open to a small river. The bank was about eight or nine feet high, and there was no access to the water on that side, but on the opposite side there was a sloping beach on which we noticed several alligators. The grass in this place was luxuriant, and our guide, the old negro, told us that we might rest and recruit ourselves here as long as we liked, secure from interference from any one, for the " Isla " was known only to himself of living men; every one else believed that the forest extended right up to the river's bank. It could not be seen from the river as the river was not navigable, and the opposite bank, and the country on the other side, was an impassable swamp for miles. He gave some further information to Ryan, the nature of which we were not aware of, and after siesta he left us.

CHAPTER XVII.

Shooting deer and pigeons—A pigeon-roost—Ball practice on alligators—Surprised by the enemy—A cavalry charge—Thrown from my horse and roll into the river—A swim for life—Our leader and half our number missing—Escape through a swamp.

AFTER exploring all round this place we felt satisfied that there was no exit or entrance but the pathway we had cut ourselves, and we believed that the old negro had told the truth when he said that it was unknown to any one but himself, and that he had not been there for years. The fact of there being no entrance to it, until we cut one through the wood, showed plainly that no one had been there for a long time.

A week's rest at this place made a wonderful improvement in both men and horses, for although we were close to a swamp on the other side of the river, we were troubled very little with mosquitoes, for there was, generally, a current of air from the wood into the open, that in a great measure kept these pests away from us.

We cut a sloping pathway in the bank of the river so as to be able to water the horses and bathe them, and we would have liked to enjoy a swim ourselves, but we were afraid of the alligators. We had some maize and a few cooking utensils that we brought with us from the plantation, but as there were no plantains or bananas to be had here, we were obliged to look about for some other means of provisioning ourselves. The first evening of our arrival we noticed several flocks of parrots, parroquets, and other birds fly over our heads, coming from the swamp across the river, to settle in the trees for the night, and here, we thought, is a good supply of meat if we can only shoot them; so we immediately started to make small shot out of our rifle bullets, and we succeeded fairly well. We almost lived entirely on these birds; but as we got stronger we extended our shooting excursions, and went through the opening in the wood and out on the outside savanna after deer. The deer were easily approached, and probably had never seen man before, for we were in an uninhabited part of the island, and the first day that we went out we shot seven; and although they were small we had to leave one of them behind, for there were only six in the party, and one each was as much as we could manage to bring back to camp. Ryan was surprised at our success, and a few days after we organised a larger party, with spare horses to bring home the game; but it was not so successful. We only killed three, and a few large blue pigeons, and experience taught us that the success of our shooting parties was generally in inverse proportion to their number. One day I got permission from Ryan to remain outside for a few days' shooting; he was very fond of pigeons, as we all were, for they were the best food we had tasted, but we shot very few of them, as they generally flew high. Morning and evening they passed over our heads in immense flocks, going and returning from the country beyond the swamp, but always flying too high for us. Judged from the height at which they flew, their roosts were some distance away in the forest on the other side of the savanna, and by going through the belt of wood that intervened between our encampment and the savanna, in the evening, we could watch for them, and see where they went to roost.

I took with me four men, Ashton, Bennet, Wyelie, and Ambrosio, a Cuban, and after siesta we saddled our horses and led them through the forest. As soon as we were clear of the timber we mounted and galloped straight across the open, until we got within a quarter of a mile of the forest, when we pulled up, loosed girths, and sat down to wait for the pigeons.

In the evening came the pigeons, flying over a

little to the right of us, and we watched them settle down in the trees, and then we mounted our horses and rode to the edge of the timber; but it was too late to make any progress in opening a road that night, so we satisfied ourselves with what food we had with us, and after tying out our horses we settled down on the ground to sleep until daylight.

We were astir in the morning long before the pigeons, and heard the noise that they made long before they came in sight, and we were prepared for them with our rifles loaded with small shot. As they flew past, low enough to be within range, we rattled into them, bringing them down in dozens; they flew so close together that it would have been impossible to miss them, and there must have been hundreds of thousands of them.

They were just far enough away to allow the shot to scatter with the best effect, for after a very few shots we had nearly a hundred lying on the ground, and I did not think it well to kill any more just then, so we started to light a fire and broil some of them on our ramrods for breakfast. After breakfast we tied up the dead birds, and loaded them on a horse, and I sent Bennet with them to the "Isla," while I and the other three men opened a way through the forest to the pigeon-roost. An hour's work brought us to comparatively open timber, where we could get along without having to cut our way with the sabre, and we soon reached the roost. All along, for a width of over a hundred yards, and a length farther than we could see, the trees were leafless and dead. The ground underneath was covered with a thick layer of the birds' dung, and nothing green was to be seen. And here, in the midst of a tropical forest, surrounded by a vegetation so rank that one could not advance a yard without cutting his way, was a strip of ground, of indefinite length, turned into a complete desert.

The next day we were joined by six or seven men from the encampment, who arrived in the midst of a heavy downpour of rain, and after living four days at the pigeon-roost, feeding on the birds, we returned to the "Isla" loaded with them. We saw some deer on our return across the savanna, but we were too heavily laden to go after them.

Everybody was kept busy next day cleaning and drying the birds in the sun, and the day following we practised with ball cartridge on the alligators basking on the opposite shore.

When we first came here we cut a *corral*, or horse-yard, in the forest, and the entrance to it could be closed by putting a sapling across the opening. The horses were allowed to run loose all day and feed in the open, and drink from the river at discretion; but there was always a man on duty to look after them. Whenever we wished to catch them, the horse guard drove them up and shut them in the corral, where we could easily catch them. During the hottest part of the day the horses came up themselves to seek the shade, and walked into the corral, where they remained switching their tails about until well on in the afternoon, when they marched out to feed again. We also built huts for ourselves of branches of trees, and thatched them with long grass; but few of the men used them, we slept outside, except when a shower of rain drove us under cover. The huts were built near the horse corral, and just inside a salient point of the wood that jutted out into the *potrero*, or pasture ground, dividing it, or rather partly dividing it, into nearly two equal parts. The place was selected by Ryan, and from it we had a view of both parts of the pasture ground and the opening at the river.

About eight or ten days after our expedition to the pigeon-roost, on a hot afternoon when we were all sleeping the siesta, stretched out lazily, dreaming in the shade, the horse guard startled us by shouting that the enemy were coming in down near the river. In a moment we were on our feet and looking rather stupefied and frightened. Ryan quietly asked if the horses were in the corral, and on being told that they were, for luckily for us they had not yet gone out to feed, he ordered us to saddle and mount immediately. I took a glance towards where the enemy were said to be coming in, before I went to obey the order, and I noticed that they were coming in by the only way that they could come in, the pathway which we had cut, and I then ran towards the horse corral. I saddled up as quickly as I could, and saw that Ryan's horse was saddled and ready for him; but while saddling up I was puzzled thinking what he intended to do. How are we going to get out of this place on horseback? The only way out was in the possession of the enemy, and even if it were open we could not ride out, but would have to walk through the wood, leading our horses.

Ryan remained watching the enemy from the huts; we could not see them from the corral, but he had a good view of both parties, and as soon as he saw that we were mounted he ran to the corral and jumped on to his horse, then turning towards us he spoke a few hurried words, telling us that the enemy, to the number of twenty-six men, had come through with their horses, and instead of advancing or sending some men to reconnoitre, or marching further up through the *potrero* to look for us, their leader had drawn them up in line across the horse path that we had cut in the river bank leading to the water, and quite close to the river. "From that," said Ryan, "I infer that there are more of them yet to come through, and this troop is waiting orders from their superior officer. This is our opportunity and we must take it; it is our only chance. We must go right through these fellows and into the river; if your horse won't jump when you reach the bank, leave him and jump yourself, there is no other way out of here; when you get into the water strike out for the other side, and when you get there, run up to the back of the beach and lie down in the swamp, and wait for the next move." While he was speaking I saw him unbuckle his revolver and throw it away, and I followed his example, throwing away also my blanket, belt, and scabbard, and retaining only the naked sword, so that I would not be encumbered in swimming if I should be fortunate in reaching the river.

The men who had belonged to the artillery company and were armed with swords, threw away their rifles and cartouches, and I *believe* most of the others did the same. We trotted out of the corral and were formed in two short lines, those with swords in front, and hurried forward, Ryan telling us to make haste before it was too late.

All this was done in less time than I have

taken to describe it, and as we trotted out beyond the point of wood the enemy had a full view of us, as we had of them, drawn up in the position described to us by our commander. On seeing us coming towards them they made a movement as if about to execute some manœuvre, or change their position, when Ryan called on us to charge, shouting, as we broke into a gallop, to keep close together, as close as possible, and that we would be sure to break through them.

Away we went as hard as the horses could go, but in our hurry we got rather mixed, for instead of being on the flank I found myself near the middle in front, with my commander riding a little distance ahead on my left front; but we kept close enough, for I have a lively recollection, even to this day, of what I felt from the grinding of my knees against those of the men on the right and left of me, and I have never since seen a cavalry charge, even in review, without thinking of the men in the middle, and surmising how they felt about the legs, if their distances were not *very* well kept.

The shock soon came, and down went horses and men on both sides. My horse struck one of the enemy's on the shoulder, and down he went backwards with his rider in a heap, my roan stumbling and falling on the top of them, where,

I suppose, he kicked every one near him to death. I was sent flying out of the saddle with the shock, and struck the ground clear of everything, rolling over and over several times, and finally rolled off the bank into the river. When I came to the surface, I struck out for the other side, but felt impeded by a weight hanging from my right arm, and feeling with my left hand, I discovered that it was my sword that was hanging from my wrist by the sword-knot. I soon slipped it off, and swam as well as I could for the other side; but my left shoulder was very painful where I struck the ground.

I observed several men and a few horses in the water swimming, and as the men passed me easily, I realised that I was making little or no progress, owing to my stiff shoulder. Then I heard reports of musketry, and became aware of another sound in the water near me, zip—zip—zip! and then it struck me that we were being fired at. I turned my head to look back, although the action caused me pain, and I then saw the enemy on the bank loading and firing at us; the bullets striking the water close to my ears, and spattering it occasionally in my face. The groans and dying gurgle of some poor comrade swimming ahead of me, as he received his quietus from a Spanish bullet, and sank under water, helped to quicken my movements, notwithstanding my stiff shoulder, and I redoubled my efforts to reach the other side, and landed safely.

The only man who could not swim—my friend Ashton—got over without a scratch, and he was the only man who brought a horse over with him, although it was not his own, and in reality it was the horse that brought Ashton; for on seeing the horse without a rider in the water, he jumped in and caught hold of his tail, where he held on, and the horse swam across with him.

Whatever other horses fell or jumped into the water with their riders, must have returned to the same side again, after their riders were shot or drowned. One poor fellow, after making good his escape, and getting clear across the river, was shot through the back as he was running up the beach towards a little ridge, or mound, that divided the river beach from the swamp. We lay on our faces behind this ridge of ground, nine of us, while the enemy continued to fire at us for some time, but without doing us any harm. Every moment we expected to see them take the water with their horses, and cross in pursuit of us; but they did not attempt it. Probably they were afraid of the alligators that infested the river, and did not care to run the risk for the sake of the few who escaped.

I asked for the names of the men who were with me, for some of them were lying down a few yards away, and as they called them out, I knew well who were missing. Ryan, our commander, was among the missing. The brave man, whose lead I had followed since we landed on the coast, and whose example had taught me how to bear hunger, fatigue, and hardship, with patience; he with whom I had spoken only a few minutes before, and on whom we depended to guide us out of our difficulties, was gone at last! And as I thought of him and our forlorn condition, I buried my face in my hands and burst into tears.

I was recalled to myself by hearing one of my companions remark that the Spaniards had gone back from the edge of the bank, and we immediately took advantage of it to run into the swamp, where we were well covered with the tall reeds and rank swamp-grass. We waded through it all that afternoon, the water sometimes reaching to our arm-pits, and again shallowing to knee-deep. Whenever the water began to get deeper, a man went ahead, or was driven ahead, on our only horse, to explore and warn us. Many a time, on reaching a shallow place, we had to rest ourselves, for it was trying work wading through the water and mud, and even when tired, we were afraid to halt in the deeper places on account of the alligators.

As the night drew near we were still a long way from the dry land, and our horse, tired out, had to be abandoned in the swamp, for we were too fatigued to waste our strength in driving him before us, and I suppose that he fell a prey to the alligators.

The night was well advanced before we reached dry ground, and we were so done up that we squeezed some of the water out of our clothes and threw ourselves down to sleep on the first dry spot that we came to. At daylight we went towards some trees, where we hoped to find something to eat, and fortunately we were not disappointed, and we might have had flesh meat also if we had had any firearms, but we only mustered three knives amongst nine men.

All day we rested under the trees, and repaired our tattered clothing, pinning our rags together with the thorns which we found in the bush. In rolling over the ground after being thrown from my horse the day before, my uniform shirt had been torn into ribbons, from the neck to the waist, and the skin on my back and shoulders abraded, and as my back was exposed to the sun all the afternoon in crossing the swamp, it was now raw, and caused me great pain.

Some of the others were in no better condition, and while we rested here we debated our prospects and chances of escape. One young fellow, Bennet, a sailor, tore off the ragged sleeve of his shirt and gave it to me for a cap, as I had no head-covering;

the action disclosed an anchor tattooed on his arm, and it immediately suggested the idea to some one that we should make our way to the coast and travel along it, and represent ourselves as shipwrecked sailors. This might do as long as we did not fall in with any troops or any one who had met us before; in that case our gray shirts, ragged as they were, would tell on us, otherwise the idea seemed feasible, but we thought it desirable to get several days' march to the westward of where we were before putting it into practice.

CHAPTER XVIII.

Resting in the forest—Using fruit for ointment—Presence of mind, which treats of Spanish America.

ALL night long I lay awake with the pain of my back and shoulder, and at daylight I roused up Ashton to ask him if he knew of anything or could do anything for me. Poor good-natured Tom started up at once, and began to condole with me, saying: "What an unfortunate fellow you are! We never meet or get near the Spaniards but you are sure to get hurt somehow, and look at me—I get through it all without a scratch. If we only had a little oil I'd soon fix your back, but where the deuce are we going to get oil here? Perhaps there's a house not far off. Never mind, I'll see if I can't find something in the bush that will answer." And away he rushed into the wood, stooping as he passed one of the sleeping men to pull the knife out of his belt.

I walked up and down, for I could not rest

with pain, and watched and envied some of my companions who still lay sleeping on the ground. When Ashton returned he brought some alligator pears and another kind of wild fruit, of which I have never heard the name. It grows on a runner or climbing plant, and when ripe is of a pale yellow colour, and about the size of a common hen's egg. He wanted to rub the juice of this on my back; he did not know that it would do any good, but he thought that I might try it.

"There's nothing else," he said; and he thought that that should be conclusive.

"I'll try it on my arms," said Bennet. "I believe that's the way the doctors find out the use of things, by experimenting on fellows. If they cure a man, why, they're all about, and know the kind of stuff to shove into the next fellow that comes along, and if they kill him, well—they don't let on that they poisoned him; they say that he died from something with a blessed long name, that would break a fellow's jaw if he was to try and pronounce it. And that's how they find out the poisons, too. Come along here, Ashton—hang the odds! Poison or no poison, I'm going to try everything I come across, and if I get through with this job I may discover something that will make my fortune. Go on, Ashton, rub it on—they're not bad tasting things, anyway," he said, taking up one and eating it. "A fellow might as well get poisoned as be hunted about like a wild beast."

Bennet declared the remedy to be good, he said "it pinched a little but was cooling," and then every one wanted to try it, and they had to go and collect some more. There was an abundance of this fruit close at hand, and we made our breakfast of it; in fact, I lived entirely on it for the few days that we remained here, as I preferred it to the alligator pear, and I found it soothing when rubbed over my sore places.

We remained quietly here for a few days, as there was plenty of food, such as it was, and shelter, for we were on the edge of a forest with an open savanna before us, and beyond that the swamp, the river, and our old encampment; the place was secure and could not be approached very well by any one unobserved, so we rested, and dressed our sores, and talked of the past and the future. Amongst other things we criticised the action of our commander in charging on the Spaniards. Some one said that we had committed a great mistake, for if there were not more than the twenty-six men that we saw, we could have given a good account of them with our rifles without ever leaving our position; that we ought not to have charged as we did; that the right thing to do would have been to have opened fire on them whenever they appeared, and that Ryan showed a want of presence of mind when taken by surprise. That was the opinion of most of the men, but then they had forty-eight hours to think over it, and we are all wise after the battle.

Ryan had been obliged to decide immediately and under circumstances which prevented a comprehensive view of the situation. He believed that the enemy were more numerous, and that we had not seen the whole of their force; and that if we were successful at first we would have been overpowered in the end; and that making a rush through them for the river was our best chance of escape. Besides, no one could say with certainty that there were no more, and Ashton and I maintained that our commander had acted for the best under the circumstances; and this leads me to think how men are affected by surprises. Some men when taken by surprise fall back to gain time, to see and think, and to collect themselves for resistance, and to consider the odds against them; others are seized with panic and bolt and run anywhere for safety, although when they come to their senses and master their fears they may drive back and defeat the force that they ran from. This, however, does not often happen, for the leaders must be very good, and have a good deal of experience and influence with the men, to be able to check and rally them after they have once broken and run. There are others again who, when taken by surprise, without seeming to think of the consequences, rush instinctively at the enemy and engage him without weighing the odds, whether they are in their favour or against them; they think of that afterwards, if they are not wiped out completely.

Occasionally the very audacity of the resistance brings success, and they repulse the attacking party or effect their escape. Presence of mind in moments of difficulty and danger is an admirable quality, no doubt, and at critical moments it has often saved a party or a man; but presence of mind gets credit for many things where it is not due, or, rather, men get credit for presence of mind where they have only acted instinctively, on the impulse of the moment, and without a moment's thought. If the action has brought about a desirable result, the individual gets credit for presence of mind; if it fails, we hear no more about it. And this reminds me of an episode that will serve as an illustration.

Many years after the adventures related in this book, and in another part of the New World, I happened to be present with a few companions; we were in a room talking and looking at a map that lay spread out on the table before us.

I had already given my opinion, and I was standing behind a chair, with my hands resting on the back of it, while two of my companions were leaning over the map. Presently we heard a tramp of feet and a jingling of arms in the passage outside, and the door was suddenly thrown open, and an officer, with a drawn sword in his hand, stood in the doorway, and said: "You are my prisoners, gentlemen," and something else, which I did not catch, for I raised the chair that I was leaning on, and hurled it at him. He raised his sword to parry the chair; but at the same time he stepped back half a pace, just sufficient to allow me to slam the door in his face, and throw the iron bar across in the hasps.

There was no escape through the windows, even if they were not guarded, for they had iron gratings on the outside, and we did not waste time over them; but after fastening an inner door, we put out the lights, for the soldiers were trying to force the door in the passage, and were firing through it, and we raised the table on its end against the wall and climbed up, and cut a hole in the ceiling. This was only a moment's work, for the ceiling was simply canvas stretched tightly across to hide the timber of the roof, and papered over. We took off a few tiles, and were in the act of getting out on the roof, when we heard the soldiers breaking into the room below, and shouting for a light. We ran along to the end of the roof, and then down on the roof of a corridor, from which we dropped to the ground; and as we turned the first corner to get away, we came full on a soldier posted there. I was about to rush at him to overpower him, and save ourselves by preventing him from making a noise, when one of my companions shouted to him in a loud voice:

" Have they come this way?"

" No, sir," replied the soldier.

" Then they must have gone round the other way," said my companion, speaking to us; and to the soldier: " Don't you stir from there without orders."

" No, sir," said he; and we had to turn round and seek another way out, which we finally managed to do in safety.

My companions were never tired of praising what they called my presence of mind, in throwing the chair and closing the door; although I am free to say that I did it without a thought, I did it impulsively. I saw an armed enemy appear suddenly before me, and I instinctively threw the first thing at hand at him, without thinking of escape or the consequences of my act. It was only when I saw that we were rid of our visitor for a moment, and that I had got the door fastened so easily, that I began to think of escaping through the roof. Where I think real presence of mind was shown, was when one of my companions spoke to the soldier, and in a tone of voice loud enough to have been heard by any one within ten yards of us. It was risky, for he could have been heard if there had been any one about; but people who carry their lives in their hands must not hesitate to take the bull by the horns occasionally, and the fact of giving orders, and speaking in a loud tone of voice, must have allayed the soldier's suspicions, if he had any, on seeing us approach him. I and the others were about to rush on him and knock him over, as the only thing to do, and, perhaps, if we had had our way, the struggle and the noise made by the man would have served to guide our enemies on to us. However, our companion's presence of mind saved us, and saved the soldier's life; yet they always gave me the greatest credit, and were never tired of praising the presence of mind of the *Inglés*.

CHAPTER XIX.

We reach the coast—Cocoa-nuts and their owner—Shipwrecked sailors—Trinidad and Casilda—We stop in time—In rags—Hiding in the mangrove swamp—Ships in harbour—We swim off to one—Reception on board.

As soon as we felt in a condition to move we started on the march to the westward, and after three days' wandering through forests and swamps, and crossing and recrossing small streams repeatedly, we directed our steps towards the coast and some cocoa-nut trees which we saw growing there. As we drew near the trees we saw a hut close by, and walked boldly up to it with the intention of trying the effect of our shipwreck story on its inmates, but we found it unoccupied. There was the remains of a fire in the middle of the floor, with a tripod standing over it, on which sat a small black kettle. A pot, a hammock, a large rough box, a stool, and a few gourds completed the furniture of the hut, which stood out on a big patch of sand that extended a long way out from the mainland. Nothing grew near it but the cocoa-nut trees, and they grew out of the sand and almost on the beach. A sandy beach extended for miles, as far as we could see on each side, and neither on the shore nor on the sand-spit between the hut and the mainland could we see any living thing. Bennet climbed one of the trees, and threw down some cocoa-nuts, which we contrived to open with some difficulty, and made a meal of, and as the place was lonely and unoccupied we decided to pass the night there, and made ourselves at home. A negro put in an appearance in the evening, coming along the shore with an old fowling-piece over his shoulder, and a dead bird swinging in his hand. As soon as we caught sight of him we started to bury the shells and husks of the cocoa-nuts in the sand, and before he reached the hut we had removed all signs of our depredations, and were duly prepared with the shipwreck story.

He politely saluted us in Spanish, and said: "What can I offer you, gentlemen?" putting stress on the word gentlemen, and looking us all over from head to foot.

We told our tale of shipwreck—poor English sailors cast away several leagues from there, down the coast; we were the only survivors, captain and officers lost, and we were making our way along the coast to the nearest seaport. Could he tell us where we were, and the nearest port?

He heard us quietly to the end, and then ignoring the whole story he asked us if we did not belong to the insurgent forces, telling us at the same time that we had nothing to fear from him, and that we were only a few leagues from Puerto Casilda, where there were several European and American vessels at anchor.

He addressed himself directly to our Cuban companions, calling them *Paisanos,* or fellow countrymen, but they pretended not to understand him, and allowed the others of the party, in broken Spanish, to carry on the conversation, while the negro plucked his bird and prepared his supper.

He lit a fire and made a kind of stew with his bird and some sweet potatoes and yams that he took out of the big box; but he did not offer us any part of it. He gave us five large sweet potatoes, and told us that we might roast them in the embers of the fire for ourselves.

Wyelie, one of our party, got indignant at being treated in this way, saying: "Look here, boys, are we going to stand this? Nine white men to be put upon by a d—— nigger! We're masters of the situation; let's tie the nigger up, and help ourselves to the stew and whatever else he's got in that box. He's sure to run and inform on us after we leave here, if we don't."

I objected to this; we had often fared far worse,

and it would be bad policy to make an enemy of the man; besides, I believed the man to be favourable to us. He might have been more generous, but that was not his *genio*, as the Cubans say; he was probably an economical nigger, and did not wish to waste his substance on shipwrecked sailors, or insurgent soldiers, who would never make him any return. And after all, we were his guests— uninvited ones certainly—and he gave us *something* from his larder, and he may have had a dim suspicion that we were not guiltless of interfering with his cocoa-nuts; so we contented ourselves with the five potatoes, and after roasting and eating them we lay down on the beach outside, and slept soundly until morning.

At daylight we parted from the negro, still keeping up the rôle of shipwrecked sailors, and asking him in which direction Casilda lay. We went inland a few miles after leaving the hut in search of a banana or plantain grove, and after breakfasting on bananas we set about to look for a rising ground where we could climb a high tree and take a survey of the neighbourhood, and see where Casilda lay.

Our Cuban companions told us that there was a city named Trinidad de Cuba a few miles inland from Casilda port, and as they had friends near this city they intended to leave us here and travel towards it at night, where their friends would be able to find a secure hiding-place for them until better times.

They advised us not to show ourselves at any house during the day, but to try and get into Casilda in the night-time, and that we probably could easily get on board some vessel in the harbour; when the negro could see through the shipwreck story it was not likely to impose on any one else. In the afternoon we caught sight of Trinidad, Casilda, and the sea, from the top of a tree, and we bade good-bye to our Cuban companions, who started in the direction in which they expected to meet their friends, while we went towards Casilda.

As we approached the town we halted for a few minutes to rest ourselves, and to see that every man had the same story to tell; I acted as inquisitor and sat a little way apart from the others, and as each man came to me to tell his tale I had a few moments to think and to look at the men. It suddenly struck me that it would never do, that it would be certain destruction for us to attempt to enter the place. Why did I or the others not think of it before? Our appearance would condemn us at once — shipwrecked sailors! There was nothing of the sailor about us. Our legs and feet wrapped round with old Spanish uniforms! Our shirts and trousers, or what was left of them, were of a uniform gray colour—we were dressed in patriot uniform, although in rags. It would be madness to go into the town without changing our clothing; every one's eyes would be on us, with the lights from the houses glaring in our faces. If we waited until the lights were put out it would be too late to go off to any of the vessels, even if the guards in the streets or the custom-house people allowed us to pass; but they would not, they would certainly detain and lock us up until morning, when everybody could see and know who we were. No, I thought, this would be running into the lion's mouth; the best thing for us to do is to go to some place outside the town, and near the water, and swim off in the night to some of the vessels in the harbour. Ashton was the only one who could not swim, but he was plucky, and I thought that I could rig up something that would float him, and we could get him on board between us; so we turned back and directed our steps towards the water with the intention of putting this idea in execution.

But although we had a moonlight night we could not tell the nationality of any of the ships in the harbour, and we did not deem it safe to go on board of any but an English or an American vessel; and as merchant ships only fly their national colours on Sundays, we would have to wait until Sunday night before we could put our plan in execution. Then, again, the coast about the harbour was not clear and open, for it was low and swampy, and there was a thick belt of mangrove bushes growing along the shore, and out in the water, extending out in some places over a hundred yards into the sea. It seemed strange to some of us to see bushes growing in the sea-water, but it can be seen everywhere in the West Indies. We went away a few miles from Casilda and hid ourselves in some trees, where we slept until late in the forenoon of the next day.

There was plenty of food in this neighbourhood to be had for the trouble of gathering it, but we had to be very circumspect in our movements, and keep very close, as there were houses not far apart and people moving about, and that evening we thought it best to move down to the mangrove bushes by the sea, at all risks; this we managed to do unperceived by any one, and waited patiently for Sunday, passing our time in fighting the mosquitoes and in making a life-buoy out of rushes and bits of rotten wood, to enable my friend Ashton to get off.

Sunday morning came at last, and we heard the ships' bells in the harbour strike eight, and presently all the vessels had their bunting flying; we saw

Spanish, German, and American flags; the Germans were all Bremen barques, brigs, and schooners. The nearest American vessel was a barque, and we resolved to try and swim to her as soon as night came to shelter us; we carefully took her bearings with regard to the land and objects on it, and as night drew near we watched for the first stars appearing in the sky between and near her masts, as guides to us in swimming off to her.

When night came it was very dark, and we waited a couple of hours until the moon got up, and we had some difficulty in getting outside the mangroves, for they grew in water too deep to wade in, and they grew too close together to swim through them, so that it was a continual splutter-duck and scramble, and cost us time and trouble to get through with Ashton and his life-buoy. We were much longer in making our way through the mangroves than we were in swimming off to the ship.

At last we got through, and with Ashton and the improvised life-buoy under his breast and arms, we started on our swim. I swam on one side of him and Bennet on the other, and we shoved him along between us. I felt my shoulder very painful still, now that I had to use my arm in swimming, and I was doubtful of being able to swim off, and mentioned it to Bennet, when he advised me to rest it as much as possible on Ashton's buoy, and strike out with my right hand. The night was very calm, and the other four fellows were soon a good way ahead of us. Ashton made a great noise in the water trying to swim, and spurting the water out of his mouth. I noticed several shark fins sticking out of the water on all sides of us, but only once did one come near us, as we got near the barque; we swam almost under the stern of a paddle steamer, and she turned out to be the Spanish war steamer *Neptuno*. We passed so near that I read her name on her stern in large white letters. We did not then know the risk that we ran in going so close to her, but we afterwards learned that war vessels have men on the look-out all round them at night, who hail everything that passes near them. By good luck we passed her unobserved, and reached the barque in safety, and got on board with some difficulty, as the greater part of her cargo had been discharged, and she floated so high in the water that a man swimming could not reach the gangway-ladder, and we had to climb on board by the anchor-chains.

The vessel that we boarded was the *Ida Kimball*, of Boston, and as she had not completed the discharging of her outward cargo, there was a Spanish custom-house officer still living on board of her. Luckily for us, it was near midnight when we got on board, and he was below asleep in his cabin. The officers and crew were all asleep, with the exception of one man who was on anchor watch. He took us into the forecastle, and went aft to call the mate, who was lying asleep on the poop under the awning. When he came forward, he asked us who we were and where we came from; we told our story, plain and simple, but he pretended not to believe us. He said that he never heard of any rising, or of any fighting in the country, and told us that he did not believe a word of what we said, and that he thought we were convicts, or jail-birds, who had broken out of prison. He asked us where was the boat that brought us off, and when we told him that we swam off, he called us a "parcel of lying thieves," and went to look over the bulwarks for the boat that he said must have brought us off. He asked the man on anchor watch how we came on board, and even after his evidence that we swam alongside, and climbed up by the anchor-chains, and seeing us dripping wet, and the water running off our rags, and forming pools on the deck under our feet, he still pretended not to believe us, and said that any one attempting to swim off from the shore would be devoured by the sharks, as the harbour was infested with them.

He spoke about calling the captain and the

custom-house officer, and sending a boat to advise the captain of the port to have us removed from the ship. I begged him not to inform the authorities, as that would be giving us up to certain death; that we were countrymen in distress; that I was a gentleman, however disreputable my appearance; that we were exactly as we had represented ourselves; that we had not touched anything on board his vessel, nor would we. If he would kindly point out to us the nearest American or English vessel, we would quietly drop overboard again, and take our chance among the sharks in swimming to her; that surely in some ship in the harbour we would find a fellow countryman not devoid of compassion.

I had scarcely spoken the last words, when one of my companions, no longer able to control himself, passionately exclaimed:

"Look here, mate; my father is——" mentioning the name of a well-known mill-owner in New York State; "if you've never heard of him, your skipper probably has. He'll pay my passage to the States, and that of my associates also, if it's that you're after. Call your skipper, and I'll talk to him."

The mate seemed to soften down, and saying that he would acquaint the captain, he went aft. After a while he came forward again, and told us that the captain would see us in the morning, and that we were to keep below out of sight of the custom-house officer; and he ordered the man who was on watch to make coffee for us.

If our appearance did not excite pity, it certainly never would beguile confidence, for seven more disreputable-looking tatterdemalions it would not have been easy to imagine. The sleeves of our shirts only reached our elbows in ragged fringes, and some were without sleeves altogether. The bodies of all of them were more or less torn. Our heads were covered with anything from a shirt-sleeve to a few leaves tied on with a piece of agave fibre. Our trousers went no farther than the knee, some not quite so far, and all were slashed from the waist to the knee, and kept from blowing about in ribbons by pieces of fibre tied round the leg here and there, as the staves of a cask are held together by the hoops. Our feet and legs were covered with several wrappings of old uniforms, tied on with anything that came to hand, and as the cloth got worn under and about the feet, the wrappings had been gradually moved down, so that while on some they reached nearly to the knee, on others, who did not know how to economise and arrange them, they reached only a little above the ankle. Our faces were bloated and swelled from the sun and the bites of mosquitoes and other tropical insects, and all the exposed parts of our bodies, hands, arms, faces, and legs, were covered with sores. We were, in truth, a repulsive-looking set, and perhaps there was some excuse for the mate after all, in wishing to be rid of us.

Some of us had sabre, bayonet, or gun-shot wounds, not yet healed, and we were in a most deplorable condition, and probably we have to thank our youth and good constitutions for carrying us through.

CHAPTER XX.

The captain agrees to take two—He promises to place the others—Ashton and I are transferred to the *Tyrer*—The Scotch skipper—Our wretched condition—Quartered with the apprentices.

THE next morning we had an interview with the captain, who came to see us in the forecastle. He had heard our story from his mate, but he asked us a good many questions, and when he discovered that the two strongest of our party were young sailors he offered them a passage to the States in his ship, and promised to make inquiries amongst the other vessels in the harbour if any of them would take us to work our passages out of the country.

We thanked him, and he then left us and went ashore in his boat. He was as good as his word, for when he came on board in the evening there was another ship captain with him, and while they chatted together on the poop a blue woollen shirt, a pair of coarse duck trousers, and a Scotch cap for each were sent to the forecastle, and Ashton and I were told to dress ourselves in them and get into a boat that lay alongside, and that we were going on board an English barque.

Before leaving the *Kimball* we heard that the rest of our companions were to be distributed that evening in other vessels, so we shook hands with them and bade them good-bye, as we were not likely to meet again, and walked aft and down the gangway ladder into the boat; here we found two young men, the boat's crew, sitting on the thwarts and waiting for their skipper. I threw myself down in the stern-sheets, and Ashton sat down beside me; the young men in the boat looked hard at us, but did not speak, and we ourselves were not in a mood for conversation; they were ship's apprentices, although they were older than we were.

We had not long to wait before the skipper came hurrying down the ladder into the boat, and looking at us in surprise when we bade him good evening, he answered us with: " Hut-toot-toot; jump forrid and catch hold o' a oar, an' len' a haun' ta pull me abourd." Our skipper was a stout, rosy-faced Scotchman of about forty years of age, and as soon as we had settled down to our work of helping to pull him to his ship, he addressed us again, saying: "I see ye can pull a oar raight weel, an' if ye promise to behave yersels an' wark weel, an' gie a haun' at everathing tha's goin', I'll gie ye a passage to Englan' as ye air twa Breetish subjec's." I let Ashton answer him while I mechanically pulled at the bow oar.

Presently he remarked our sore and swollen faces, and exclaimed:

"Wha's wrang wi' yer heeds? Theer ah-flee swelled. Ye've no been feichtin amang yersels, ye scabby-lookin' deevils, have ye?"

Ashton reassured him, and explained that it was the effects of mosquito bites and other swamp insects.

"It's verra strange," said he, "but musketers have no siccan an effec' on me. I hope yer no bringin' ony diseese abourd ma sheep, for it'll be a verra bad spec if ye do."

When we got alongside his ship he went up the gangway ladder, and standing in the gangway shouted out: "Meester O'Brien, Meester O'Brien, I want ye here a moment," and as soon as the mate appeared he called us on deck, and then turning to the mate he said: "Here ye are, Meester O'Brien, here are twa new haun's for ye; ye can start them ta wark in the mornin' alang wi' the men. I hae promised tae gie them a passage to Englan', if they can wark, ye ken, but if they're na guid we'll pit them ashore." And then turning to us he said:

"Noo ye understaun'. Awa' ye gang forrid an' get yer suppers."

I asked for a little ointment to dress my back.

"Yer back?" said the skipper; "yer heed, ye mean. Wha' the deevil's wrang wi' yer back? Dinna think yer comin' abourd here to lie up; if ye do ye'll find yoursel' —— weel mistaken. We want no loafers abourd here."

I explained that I was healthy enough, and had neither wish nor intention to lie up, but that my back was sore from sunburn, and that the chafing of the coarse woollen shirt aggravated it and made it worse, and that if he would kindly give me a little healing ointment and a few soft rags to lay on the sore places I would give him no further trouble, and I would be ready for work in the morning.

"Come into the cabin," said he, "an' let's ha' a look at yer back."

I followed him into the cabin, the mate and Ashton bringing up the rear, and, pulling my shirt off over my head, I exposed my back to his view.

He looked at it in surprise, and exclaimed:

"Guid God Almaichty! ha' they been tryin' to flay ye alive?"

I told him that it was an abrasion of the skin and sunburn, nothing more, and that it would soon get well.

"Yes, yes, I ken how it is. Stretch yersel' across this table here, an' I'll fix ye in twa minits."

And after dressing my back he gave me an old cotton shirt, and Ashton assisted to put it on, after which I felt much easier.

"An' noo, ma man," said the skipper to Ashton, "off wi' yer sark, an' let's ha' a look at *your* back."

Ashton assured him that he was sound, and wanted nothing.

"Weel, then, away ye go on deck, and ye can live in the half-deck the noo, alang wi' the 'prentices and carpenter. The mate 'ill gie ye some auld canvas, an' ye can get some o' the men ta mak' hammocks for ye on Sunday, when there's no wark doin', if ye dinna ken how to mak' them yersel's."

The half-deck was a space of about sixteen feet by the whole breadth of the ship, and bulk-headed off from the vessel's hold, in the 'tween-decks. The entrance was in front of the poop, and just abaft the pumps near the mainmast, and the coamings of the hatchway were much higher than any of the others, so that in fine weather at sea the "booby hatch," as it was called, that fitted over all, could be lifted off completely.

In rough or rainy weather entrance and egress was obtained through a slide-over scuttle cut in the booby hatch. This was the place that Ashton and I were to be quartered in. The forward bulkhead separated it from the hold, and the after bulkhead separated it from the ship's fore cabin, where the skipper and mates took their meals. We found the ship's cook and the carpenter, with hammocks slung on the port side, and four apprentices on the starboard side; but here in port every one lived on deck. The forecastle was covered over with an awning, under which the crew ate and slept, and the poop and quarter-deck were covered with awnings also.

Two of the apprentices were Scotch, one Irish, and one English. With the exception of the English lad, who was a tall stripling on his first voyage, the others were full-grown men, and had been nearl four years at sea, and were fairly good sailors.

After a supper of soup and biscuit, Ashton and I sought out the softest planks on the deck, and lay down until morning.

CHAPTER XXI.

Loading mahogany—Dreams—Christmas—Decorating the ship—A drunken crew—The soup tureen—The skipper comes aboard—His homily to the steward.

THE vessel we were on board of was the barque *Tyrer*, of Liverpool, an old teakwood ship, and as bluff in the bows as a Dutch galliot. She was taking in a loading of mahogany and honey for London, and it was expected that she would not have her cargo completed for three weeks.

Ashton and I worked regularly every day with the crew, assisting them in heaving at the winch and hoisting the mahogany logs on board, and in lowering them down into the hold; after the first few days, when we got into the routine of the work, we got on very well, and were soon quite at home in the ship's work, and with regular food and rest, and fair treatment, my sores got rapidly better, and our heads and faces resumed their natural size, so that when we had been a week on board we began to feel quite strong again.

The apprentices were kind to us, and, sailor-like, shared their clothes and blankets with us. I used to sleep at night on deck under the awning, rolled up in a blanket, and with a coil of rope for a pillow; and about this time, when I was beginning to get strong, I used often to wake up in the middle of the night dreaming of San Jacinto, and of fighting on shore. Once or twice I woke up the men who were sleeping near me with my shouts, and they in turn woke me up, to ask me what was the matter; the same thing happened with Ashton. After one of these dreams I used to lie awake for hours—thinking and wondering if it was not all a dream.

Only two months ago we were at San Jacinto, far away to the eastward amongst the hills. I had won my chevrons, and was a sergeant of artillery in the patriot army—highly thought of by my commander—burning with zeal to distinguish myself—surrounded with hundreds of companions; and now where were they? And I, what was I?

They were all gone—nearly all dead! And I remained, a sailor boy; no, scarcely that, for had I not been told—threatened—that if I did not work well I should be turned ashore? A boy, then, on board an old timber ship, engaged in the prosaic work of helping to load logs of wood!

The skipper did not trouble us in port; he never

interfered in the work of the ship while she lay at Puerto Casilda. He spent most of his time on shore; sometimes he slept on shore, but he generally went on shore after breakfast, and did not return until night; he had a boat to attend on him constantly, and when it was not alongside the wharf ashore, it was passing between the shore and the ship.

The mate carried on the work, and always remained on board. Some days we would have no timber to load, and then he would have the crew employed on the rigging or other necessary work.

One day the topgallant masts and yards were sent up, and Ashton was sent with one of the older apprentices to the main, while I was sent with another to the fore, and we were initiated in the art and practice of sending masts aloft and crossing yards. We were kept working on the rigging with the apprentices when there was no cargo coming on board, for our friend the mate used to say that he would make sailors of us before we saw the Channel, and I think that he partly succeeded.

While the ship lay here we had Christmas, and both the skipper and the mate went on shore the evening before, and the ship was left in charge of the second mate, a Frenchman, of Dunkirk, who figured on the ship's articles as a native of Jersey. He was a young man and a smart sailor, but made too free with the men, and as soon as the mate left the ship for the shore every one seemed to think that they were at liberty to do what they chose. When night fell some one proposed to decorate the ship with green bushes for the next day, Christmas, and the second mate entered at once into the spirit of the thing; and as the gig had just come back from the shore with notice that neither captain nor mate would be coming on board that night, and with orders to send a boat for them next morning at sunrise, we felt free to do what we liked in the meantime.

Some of the crew manned the gig, and started for the mangrove bushes that fringed the shore, to cut branches to decorate the yards and mastheads. Grog had been served out in the afternoon by the second mate, and some bottles had been given to the men at supper-time to keep up their Christmas, so that when the boats shoved off, the men who remained on board the ship were in a maudlin state, staggering about the decks, or swearing eternal friendship to each other.

I went in the pinnace with Ashton, the carpenter, and a seaman. We cut a good load of bushes, and as we were returning to the ship, towing them after the boat in the water, the carpenter got very talkative. The gig was a light-pulling boat, and had a light load; but we in the pinnace, with a heavy tow, and in a large boat, made slow progress. Presently the carpenter began to sing and shout, and it became evident that the grog was beginning to rise to his head.

In coming off from the mangrove bushes, we had to pass the *Kimball*, but leaving her a long way to our left. However, the tide, although weak, set our boat with its heavy load of towing bushes down near her, and the carpenter remarking it, asked what ship was that? Ashton replied that it was the vessel that we swam off to, when we made our escape from the shore.

He had heard the story of our reception on board the *Kimball*, and he could not let the opportunity pass of expressing his opinion of the mate's conduct. He hailed the ship, and on being replied to, he asked if the mate was on board, and when he was answered in the affirmative, he shouted out:

"Tell him to put his mug over the side for a moment, I want to talk to him; and bring a lamp—bring two lamps. I want to get a good look at the hangman that tried to sell his poor starving countrymen to the Degos for ten dollars."

This was a pure invention of his own.

The mate of the *Kimball* had the good sense not to answer or to take the slightest notice of him, and he went on abusing the mate while

DECORATING THE SHIP.

the boat was within hail. It was useless to try and stop him, he had too much grog on board to be amenable to reason; so that all we could do was to pull as hard as we could, and get the boat out of ear-shot as soon as possible. He accused the mate of every crime and meanness that he could think of or invent, and at last sat down in the boat, finishing his tirade by wishing him good-night, with an expression the reverse of complimentary to his maternal parent.

When we got on board our own vessel, we found the crew in various stages of drunkenness; but all were more or less busy in decorating the ship. The gig, with her load of green bushes, had arrived half an hour before us, and the men had them stuck everywhere. The second mate himself went aloft with a big branch, and managed, although half-drunk, to reach the main royal masthead, where he lashed it; and the rest of the crew, who were no better, carried branches to the extremity of every spar in the ship, and fastened them there.

The cook and steward had a private party of their own in the galley, where they sat with closed doors, drinking rum punch, and were deaf to all appeals for admission from those on deck outside.

The second mate and the carpenter had arranged to have a quiet little booze of their own in the after cabin, and sent to the galley for hot water;

but there was none for them. The fellows inside refused to let any one in or to open the door; so they had to content themselves without it. *They* also shut themselves up in the after cabin, and putting some rum into a soup tureen, proceeded to burn it.

Charley, an English lad, and the youngest apprentice, was kept running about attending on them until they had got all that they required collected together on the cabin table, when the second mate dismissed him, with a tin of currant jam and some cabin biscuits.

Ashton, Charley, and I, were the only sober individuals on board the ship that night, and we saw most of the game. We sat round the after skylight, eating the jam and biscuits, and after a while we got inquisitive, and wished to know what the pair below were doing. The after skylight was round, and covered on top with mahogany. The sides were of thick glass that we could not see distinctly through; but the binnacle was fixed on top, and by lifting off the binnacle lamp, and tilting the compass to one side, we could look down on the table, and see our gentlemen enjoying themselves.

While we watched them the tureen, which was of pewter, got heated above the line of flame of the burning spirit and melted, and suddenly fell over to one side, letting the rum run all over the table. We saw them mopping it up, and, replacing the binnacle lamp, we moved away off the poop and went forward, as we expected to see them come on deck after their mischance, and we wished to be out of their way, and not give them cause for thinking that we had been watching them.

The barque had a topgallant forecastle, or raised deck, forward, under which the crew slept, and, to be out of the way of some drunken fellows who were staggering about on the main deck and enjoying themselves, as they called it, singing each one in a different key, we mounted the forecastle and seated ourselves on the fife-rail, where we could overlook the deck and see everything going on without being obliged to take part in it.

We were just in time to witness another nautical manœuvre—a veritable cutting-out.

Two drunken sailors who had exhausted their supply of grog, and had tried every means of adding themselves to the cook's party in the galley without success, determined, as they could not get in, to cut the others out. One of them climbed on the roof of the galley, and, unshipping the upper part of the funnel, he wantonly threw it overboard. The other fellow, after several ineffectual attempts, managed to draw a bucketful of water and handed it up to him, and he deliberately emptied it down the galley chimney.

The next moment we could hear a great commotion amongst the party inside, and a rattling and shaking of the doors, hurrying to get them open, which they finally succeeded in doing, and rushed out on deck covered and nearly smothered with ashes.

The man on the roof had made his final exertion for that night, for, overcome with the grog he had drunk, he lay back where he sat on the galley roof and slept until morning, while his accomplice, leaning against the bulwarks in the shadow of the fore-rigging, and with a drunken leer on his face, watched the cook, who was as drunk as any of the others, accuse every one that he met on deck. He never thought of looking on the roof of his galley, where the culprit was stretched out quietly sleeping.

While this was going on on the port side of the deck, we saw two figures appear on the poop and come forward to inquire into the row that the cook and his friends were making. They were the second mate and the carpenter.

The carpenter kept the cook in conversation while the second mate ran aft and down into the cabin, from which he appeared presently with one hand behind his back, and, coming along on the starboard side, he rushed into the now open galley for a moment, and then hurried back to the poop again and began calling "Chips! Chips!"—the name the carpenter is known by on board ship—as if he had never left the poop.

He had taken the damaged tureen and laid it on the galley stove, probably thinking that the cook would find it there in the morning when he was sober, and think that he himself or his friends had left it there; but he was in such a hurry that he forgot to put the melted side of the tureen, and bottom up, next the fire, and as the stove happened to be almost cold, the cook found it when he came to light his fire in the morning with the melted part uppermost —the part that had not been in contact with the stove—and he knew at once that some one had been trying to play a trick on him, and his first exclamation on seeing it was: "Hello! who's melted the tureen?"

The first salute I had from the cook next morning when I went to get my coffee at his galley, was: "Look here, young fellow. Do *you* know who the swab is that tried to sell me a dog?"

"Sell you a *dog*, cook, how? What do you mean?"

"Oh! you needn't pretend to be so d——d green. You know d——d well what I mean."

And taking the tureen in his hand, and turning it round, while he held it up before my face, he said: "There's what I mean; and I mean to find out the d——d sweep that did it. Oh! I'll find him out before the end of the voyage, you'll see if I don't."

I was in the boat that went ashore on Christmas morning to bring off the skipper and the mate; we had to wait for over an hour at the wharf before they made their appearance, and as we pulled out into the harbour, and came in sight of the ship, the skipper remarked the green branches with which she was decorated, and called the mate's attention to it, saying: "What the deel have they been doin' to the ship?"

"Oh," said the mate, "that's Quebec fashion for Christmas."

When we got alongside the second mate was at the gangway to receive us, looking quite fresh and clean, and when we got on deck we found that he had managed to muster hands enough to wash the decks and remove all traces of the night's debauch, for everything looked neat and tidy. There was no one in sight about the decks with the exception of the cook bustling about the galley-door. It was Christmas Day and there was no work going on, so the men were sleeping off the effects of last night's jollification.

They had plum-duff and a glass of grog at dinner, and by that time everybody seemed to have recovered from their spree.

The cabin dinner was served on the fore cabin

skylight that day under the awning, where the skipper and his mates sat; the same awning extending to the mainmast, and covering the part of the deck where we sat with the carpenter and apprentices having our dinner. As we were within ear-shot of the party on the poop, although out of their sight, we heard all the conversation that went on there. Even below in the half-deck we could hear through the bulkhead the conversations carried on in the fore cabin, and very often we knew beforehand what work it was proposed to do on the passage home.

While we sat on the deck eating our dinners, some of us with our backs against the booby-hatch, and others leaning against the break of the poop or the after capstan, the deck serving as seat and table for all, the steward came aft from the galley with the tureen full of soup, and we all looked in surprise at it as he passed us to see how he had repaired it, and made it possible to hold anything liquid. He had fixed it up with splinters of wood and marled all over with spun yarn, like a sailor's tobacco plug.

The carpenter looked at us and winked as the steward mounted the poop ladder, as much as to say: Listen to the skipper exploding when he sees the tureen.

It was not long in coming, for the steward had

scarcely laid it down when, the skipper's eye catching it, he broke out with:

"Hello! wha's wrang wi' the tureen?"

"I don't know, sir," said the steward; "the cook found it on his galley-stove this morning, he thinks that somebody put it there; he doesn't know how it got there, and I don't know either, for I never took it to the galley. Somebody must have put it on the stove."

"Yes," said the skipper, turning the tureen round and examining it all over, "the deil a doot aboot it, an' somebody pit aw that spun yarn aboot it too, I ken that brawly." Then looking the steward in the face for a few moments, and shaking his head slowly, for he had not quite recovered from his own booze on shore, he said slowly: "Ech, mon, but ye maun ha' been verra far gone in liquor, the pair o' ye, when ye ken naething aboot it. Howsomever, I'll dock the preece o' it aff yer wages, an' that'll eempress it weel on yer memory, an' larn ye ta keep yer weather ee liftin' the nex' time ye gang on the fuddle. Ye can tell that auld deevil o' a cook that as ye were fu' togither ye maun be dool togither, an' pay it between ye."

We who were in the secret, and were watching the skipper through the bucket-rack as he lectured the steward, thought that this was hard on the cook and the steward, but they were not liked by the men and no one pitied them. No one knew, but we who saw it thrown overboard, what had become of the galley funnel, and the carpenter had to make a new one out of a piece of sheet-iron.

A few weeks afterwards, when we were at sea on the passage home, it was my watch below one afternoon, and I lay in my hammock swinging gently with the motion of the ship, when I overheard the skipper and the mate talking in the cabin. The mate said:

"I found out what became of the galley funnel, sir; I got talking to the boy Charley, and asked him what part he took in the play on the night of Christmas Eve, and I got out of him that he saw a man get on the galley roof and unship the funnel and throw it overboard, but he won't say who the man was. He says that it was too dark for him to recognise him."

"Ah, weel," said the skipper, "ye may depend upon it 'twas the auld cook himsel'—whatever objec' he had. Maybe the auld carl was afeerd he'd spoil the dinner yon day, an' wanted to mak' oot that the want o' a funnel to his gelly was the cause o' it."

"He'd scarcely do that, sir," said the mate.

"Hoot-toot, mon, ye dinna ken him as weel as I do; ye've no been shipmates wi' him before, as I hae. Yon auld carl, when he's in liquor, will dae some unaccoontable things."

And so the cook got credit for another performance with which he had nothing to do, all through not keeping his weather eye open when he went on what the skipper termed "the fuddle."

CHAPTER XXII.

Sailors' songs—The forecastle poet—Our comrades shout farewell—Go on shore—Trinidad—Speak with Spanish soldiers—The war over—Drunken Englishmen—Cuba, good night.

EVERY one was very quiet on board the ship on Christmas Day; the skipper went to sleep in his cot in the after cabin, after dinner; the mates lay stretched on the lockers or hen-coops on the poop, sleeping and reading alternately, and the crew passed the day in a similar manner; an odd one might have been found mending his clothes.

But in the cool of the evening they mustered on deck, and after supper they broke into song on the forecastle head. Sailors' songs are not as a rule edifying, and there is as little to admire in them as in the life of the sailor himself; still the poetic spirit sometimes shows itself even in a ship's forecastle, and we were not without it on board the *Tyrer*.

There was an ordinary seaman amongst the crew who could string some very fair verses together, and the men—particularly the younger ones and the apprentices—delighted in singing them.

The songs were about the ship, or some ship that they had once sailed in, or the captain, officers, or owners, and their peculiarities. The words were generally adapted to some well-known air with a good chorus, and were often more witty than polite.

There was one to the tune of "The fine old English Gentleman," commemorating the cook and his performances, of which I can only recall the two first stanzas. It was called:

THE FINE (OR VILE) OLD ENGLISH COOK.

    I'll sing to you a good new song,
      Made by a young chap's pate,
    Of a vile old *cocinero*
      That sailed with us of late.
    His hair was gray and he had arrived
      At an old man's estate;
    But he had a rotten heart within,
      With lies and treachery great.
Chorus by all hands:
      This vile old *cocinero*,
      The Judas of modern times.

    He like a crawling serpent sneaks
      Into the Captain's room;
    And while he pretends to pet the dogs,
      He sucks the demi-john.
    In whisky, brandy, rum, or gin,
      It matters not a whiz,
    He'll drink until he is dead drunk,
      Then swear he teetotal is.
      This vile old *cocinero*,
      The Judas of modern times.

There was another, written on the ship's voyage out, a great favourite with the men, as it had a rattling tow-row-row chorus, and an accompaniment of stamping feet on the deck, and was one of the least objectionable. I heard it for the first time on that Christmas night, and it is a fair specimen of our forecastle poet's work.

THE TYRER.

I'll sing to you about this barque,
    The *Tyrer* she is named, sir;
She is a stout old teak-built craft,
    From Liverpool she hails, sir.
She is a splendid monthly boat,
    Runs five knots before a gale, sir,
And if we don't run short of grub,
    We're bound to beat the mail, sir.
Chorus: Tow-row-row, right-fol-de-diddle-lol-de-row-row-row.

Our Captain's name is Henderson,
    A Scotchman, you perceive, sir;
And from his accent we believe
    He comes from about Dundee, sir.
He is a decent upright man,
    A better we don't desire, sir;
With tact and right good seamanship
    He navigates the old *Tyrer*.
        Tow-row-row, etc.

Our chief mate is an Irishman,
    A rollick and a funster;
His name it is O'Brien,
    And he belongs to Munster.
He has a kind of roaring way,
    Not unlike a Yankee firer,
But he'd better mind his p's and q's
    On board the old barque *Tyrer*.
        Tow-row-row, etc.

We've got a second greaser, too,
   A kind of English-Frenchman,
Although we see in working ship,
   He's always proved a staunch man.
He's very good at going aloft,
   And orders us to go, sir,
But we know —— well, he's like ourselves,
   He'd rather go below, sir.
               Tow-row-row, etc.

Our carpenter he is a true-born
   Son of Erin's Isle, sir ;
He is a man in all his parts,
   And meets you with a smile, sir.
He'll help a friend, a foe he'll fight,
   Of righteous laws an admirer ;
Long may he wield his broad axe
   Round the old decks of the *Tyrer*.
               Tow-tow-row, etc.

Our cook, a little Guernsey man,
   He's doctor * of his trade, sir ;
Though from drinking too much grog ashore,
   Three days in bunk was laid, sir.
He with a rod of iron rules
   All boiling pots and chalice ;
The ladle is his sceptre,
   And the galley is his palace.
               Tow-row-row, etc.

There's Daddy old, and old Blow Cold,
   And Sam, and Niel, and Jack, sir,
And Davy with his shipmates
   Tom and Alick at his back, sir ;
A Dublin sprig, two little pigs,
   And then to keep us merry,
We've a Yankee packet sailor
   That hails from Londonderry.
               Tow-row-row, etc.

---

* Cooks on board ship are called " Doctor " by the crew, as they call the carpenter " Chips," and the sailmaker " Sails."

There's Charley, too, we've got on board,
  He was his mother's pet, sir ;
His head is like a scupper nail's,
  But he may get smarter yet, sir.
And we had a little stowaway,*
  God rest his little bones, sir !
The other night he tumbled overboard,
  And went to Davy Jones, sir.
            Tow-row-row, etc.

The first week after we set sail,
  In the Channel we knocked about, sir ;
'Twas tack and wear, contrary gales,
  Pump ship, and sharp look-out, sir.
We were often called to shorten sail,
  But we quickly went about, sir,
For whilst the reefs were turning in,
  The grog was turning out, sir.
            Tow-row-row, etc.

But now we've caught the north-east trades,
  They softly waft us on, sir,
And Cuba's sunny southern isle
  We hope to see ere long, sir.
Let every one his duty mind,
  Nor figure in the log-oh,
And when it comes to reef topsails,
  That we may get our grog-o.
        Tow-row-row, right-fol-de-diddle-lol-de-row-
        row-row.

A few days after Christmas, on one bright morning, a smart-looking American brigantine, or hermaphrodite-brig, as Americans prefer to call vessels of that rig, came sailing down the harbour

* A boy fell overboard from aloft one dark night when reefing topsails, and was lost. " Davy Jones's locker "—the bottom of the sea.

on her way to sea, and some one on her decks shouted something as she passed astern of us. I paid no attention to it at the time, as I was heaving away at the winch, helping to hoist a log of mahogany from the raft alongside; but in the evening, after working hours, and when we were all together at supper, Ashton spoke about it, and asked me if I had heard them. The shouts came from two of our old comrades who had swum off with us to the *Kimball*, on that memorable night when we made good our escape from the shore. They shouted a farewell to us, and wished us soon to be homeward-bound like themselves.

At last we finished loading, and then all hands were busy getting down derricks, battening down and securing the hatchways; bending sails and reeving running-gear, lashing the spare spars, filling the tank and water casks with fresh water from the shore, and when the water was all on board, hoisting in and securing the long-boat and the pinnace, and getting everything ready for sea. The ship was unmoored—that is, one anchor was hove up; and on a Saturday evening we lay riding at single anchor, ready for sea, and we were to sail on the following Monday.

On Sunday morning two of the apprentices were allowed to go on shore on liberty, and I asked permission to accompany them. They were

I GO ON SHORE.

going under charge of an old sailor called Ross, and I was anxious to try and find out the fate of my old companions in arms; to try and learn if there was any possibility of any of them being still alive, for some were supposed to have escaped with Wingate; or if dead, to learn their fate; for although there were some of them of whom, perhaps, the world was well rid, there were many good and gallant souls among them, true as steel, and deserving of a better fate.

The skipper advised me to remain on board, saying that he thought that I had had quite enough of the shore, and he was surprised that I should ever wish to set foot on it again; however, as I begged so hard and seemed so eager, he did not object, and we were pulled ashore after breakfast in the gig with himself.

When we landed at the wharf, he gave me a silver dollar, and a parting injunction to be sure and get back and be ready to go on board at sundown, as the ship would sail before daylight next morning.

I went straight from the wharf to the railway station, for there was a short line connecting the city of Trinidad de Cuba with the port Casilda, and overruling old Ross's proposal to adjourn to the nearest *pulperia*, or grog-shop, for what he called "a smile," I brought them all with me, and we took tickets for Trinidad. I could speak a little Spanish, and as my companions depended on me to act as interpreter for them in making their purchases, I led them where I chose.

When we arrived at Trinidad, Ross, who was sent by the skipper to take care of us, went into the first grog-shop near the station, and I left him there with one of the apprentices, while I went with the other young man, who was my nautical instructor on board the ship, to prosecute my inquiries through the town.

I had no fear of being recognised by any one, for I was now quite the sailor, in blue frock and white trousers, and a black silk waterproof cap on my head, and with my arm linked in Sam's, my companion, we strolled boldly up the street.

An old gentleman beckoned to us from the opposite side of the street, and when we crossed over to meet him, he spoke to us in English, asking us where we belonged to; he told us where the English Consul lived, if we wished to call on him; but we didn't. He remarked that my black head-covering was unsuitable for the tropics, and advised us to walk always on the shady side of the street, and that I—he addressed himself particularly to me as the youngest — should be very careful that I did not get sun-stroke, as I looked a soft youth fresh from Europe.

I felt nettled at being taken for a soft youth. The old gentleman little suspected that, soft as I looked, I had done several months' campaigning in the island, and had marched many a day in the sun, at times half-naked; probably I had gone through more hardships in the past few months than he had in the fifty years of his life. He was an American gentleman, apparently over fifty, and at first he took us for countrymen of his own.

After some further conversation we asked him if there were any Spanish soldiers in Trinidad, and if he could direct us to a barrack.

He looked surprised at our request, and asked us what we wanted with Spanish soldiers.

We told him that our ship was to sail the next day, and that we would like to be able to say that we had seen them.

"Oh," he said, "you might have seen them down at the port any day, without coming up here; however, you haven't far to go, for there's a barrack in the next street, round the corner."

After thanking him we went in search of the barrack, and soon found it, for at the gate I recognised the well-known Spanish uniforms.

There was a sentry at the gate and several men standing about, and some sitting on a bench inside the gateway.

I hailed them with "Buenos dias, amigos." And

T

Sam and I were immediately surrounded by the soldiers when they heard me address them in Spanish, and they invited us in, and pressed us to sit down.

We accepted their invitation, and I carried on a conversation with them as well as I could in my broken Spanish.

I still had the dollar that the skipper gave me, for Ross paid for our train, and I gave it to one of the soldiers, and sent him to buy wine to treat his companions; and as they got talkative I gradually worked the conversation round to the war, asking them if they had been engaged in it.

They gave me to understand that they had not, but that part of their regiment, stationed in another part of the island, was engaged at one time.

When I asked how the war was going on, with the object of finding out whether the insurgents still held out in the mountains or were dispersed, and the resistance to the Government forces completely collapsed, they told me that it was all over: "No hay mas; está concluida toda" (There is no more, it is all finished), they said.

I asked what became of "Los patriotas y los Americanos" (The patriots and Americans), as we were in the habit of calling ourselves. The soldiers, with a sneer on their faces, looked significantly at each other when I made use of these names, and one of them—a *Cabo,* or corporal—laid his hand on my shoulder, and putting his mouth close to my face, as if to impress his answer more forcibly on me, shouted : " No hay tal, patriotas ni Americanos " (There are no such patriots nor Americans), and asked me where I had heard them called by these names.

I immediately saw that I was on the wrong tack, and as I could not give him a satisfactory answer I pretended not to understand him, and when he repeated the question, and the other soldiers seemed to take an interest in hearing my answer, by crowding round me, I disappointed them all by saying, " No entiendo " (I don't understand). I understood and heard well enough the remark that one of the soldiers made to another, in an undertone, as he moved away from me to take his seat again : " No es tan tonto " (He's not such a fool).

The corporal asked us if we were Americans or English, and he seemed better pleased when we told him that we were English, and belonged to a ship in the port of Casilda ; that we were ashore for a day's liberty, and that our ship would sail for England next day.

He then told us that the patriots and Americans, so called, were only bands of pirates and assassins, and that the Government troops had soon put an end to them, they were all taken and destroyed, and the country made safe.

I said nothing to this, but I wondered in my own mind if these men ever heard of the fight at the *ingenio*, the sugar-mill, where we defeated and dispersed the Spanish forces, although they were superior to us; or of the battle in the wood, where the Spanish troops were defeated by a third of their number of patriots and lost two of their guns. Or did they ever hear of the assault and capture of San Jacinto by the patriots, and the repulse of their troops in two attempts to retake it?

There was no information to be had from these men, and I had my trouble for nothing, and spent my only dollar to no purpose. The soldiers knew less than I did, and Sam and I left them and went in search of old Ross and his companion. We looked in at all the drinking places without being able to find them, until late in the afternoon; when we had given up hope of finding them, and were going towards the station to catch the train and reach Casilda by sundown, we saw a crowd in front of a doorway, and going over to see what was the cause of it we found Ross among them, drunk, and abusing the people round him, who stood laughing and jeering at him. Luckily for him, they did not understand the left-handed compliments that he was paying them in English. He was offering to fight any "mongrel" in the crowd, or any two of them if he got fair play. He accused them, or some one among them, of stealing a dollar from him, and swore repeatedly that he would not leave the place until he got it; no, not if he had to stay there until morning.

I asked Sam if he had a dollar, to give it to him and get him to the station before the train left. But Sam said: "Not I! Give him a dollar, indeed! No, but I'll give him something else that will fetch him," and making his way through the crowd, he went up to old Ross and said: "Hello, you drunken old fool, what row are you kicking up here? Fight, eh! what are you talking about fighting for? Why, you can't walk! Here, I'll give you all the fighting you want," and squaring out at him he gave Ross a good stiff blow with his fist, and immediately turned round and walked smartly away towards the station, followed by Ross in a zigzag course, and a hooting, shouting crowd of negroes and mulattoes; Ross calling on Sam to stand his ground like a man, and the mob shouting "Ingleses borrachos" (drunken Englishmen) after us until we reached the station, where we found the other apprentice. The railway cars had galleries or balconies round them on the outside, and we had some difficulty in preventing our drunken shipmate—the man who was sent to look after us —from going out there to address the people and deliver himself of his opinion of them. He told every one near him, over a dozen times, that he was no Spaniard, but "good old Jack Ross, a true-born Lancashire man." Some soldiers got into the train before starting, and we partly succeeded in keeping Ross quiet by telling him that they were looking for a drunken Englishman that was shouting and making a noise in the station. We arrived at the wharf by sundown, according to appointment with the skipper, but we had to wait until late at night before he was ready to go off. At last he made his appearance with the pilot who was to take us to sea in the morning, and we pulled off to the ship.

CHAPTER XXIII.

Getting under weigh—Homeward-bound—Sailors' shanties—
At sea—The Isle of Pines—Cape San Antonio.

THE next morning before daylight all hands were turned out to weigh anchor; round went the windlass cheerily to the sailors' rousing chorus, "Hurrah, my boys, we're homeward-bound," and long before the first streak of light appeared in the sky to the eastward the mate, who stood on the forecastle between the knight-heads watching the chain cable rattling inboard, shouted to the skipper, who walked the poop with the pilot:

"Anchors short stay apeak, sir."

"Avast heaving; away aloft, loose sails."

In a few minutes the gaskets were cast off and made up, and the white canvass dropped loose from every yard and hung simply by the clew-lines and bunt-lines, and as the men reached the deck the skipper's voice was heard shouting:

"Sheet home the main topsail." Followed immediately by the mate's: "Sheet home the foretopsail, port watch; oh! belay. Stretch along the tops'l halyards there, my hearties. Hoist away—slack off the braces."

The foretopsail rose off the cap with many jerks, and gradually got stretched out to its full height to the topmast head to the music of a "shantie," or song, given out by the carpenter, who happened to be the "shantie man" on this occasion.

Sailors' *shanties*—probably a corruption of chanting—or hauling choruses, not songs, are generally improvised by the "shantie man" who gives them out. The choruses are old and well known to all sailors, but between each pull and chorus the "shantie man" has to improvise the next line, or compose the "shantie" as he sings it. It is true there is not much in them, and any words or expression, no matter how absurd or incongruous, will answer as long as they rhyme with the line before. Although they are often without sequence they are not without music, and are as inspiriting to the sailor as the fife and drum is to the soldier. On one occasion at sea, after reefing the foresail in a gale, the united efforts of the whole crew were unable to board the foretack, or get it hauled down to its place on the cathead, until the mate of the watch called out: "Strike up a shantie there, one of you men." The "shantie" was struck up; the chorus was like a shout of defiance at the elements. It was fighting the gale, and was as inspiriting as a cavalry charge, and perhaps as hazardous. I enjoyed it, although every now and again a sea would break over the bows, drenching and blinding every one. The mate's voice would be heard shouting encouragingly to the men at each pull: "Well done, down with it, men, it must come; time the weather roll, bravo;" and at every shout of the chorus the men threw their whole weight, with a will, into the foretack, and down it came inch by inch steadily, and after a fierce struggle the tack was belayed and the crew were victorious.

The "shantie" sung this morning on getting under weigh and setting the topsails, we often heard on the passage to England, and is a good specimen of sailors' "shanties;" the men have breathing time to collect their strength and prepare themselves for the pull, while the "shantie man" is giving out the verse. At every repetition of the word "Hilo" in the chorus the men all pull together with a jerk, hoisting the heavy yard and sail several inches at every pull. "Give us 'Hilo,' Chips," the men said to the carpenter, and he began. The preliminary "Oh" long drawn out at the beginning of each verse was to gain time to improvise the verse :

Oh-o, up aloft this yard must go,
                Chorus by all hands : Hilo, boys, hilo !
I heard our bully mate say so.
                                Hilo, boys, hilo !

Oh-o, hilo, bullies, and away we go,
                                Hilo, boys, hilo !
Hilo, boys, let her roll, o-he-yho.
                                Hilo, boys, hilo !

Oh-o, I knocked at the yellow girl's door last night,
                                Hilo, boys, hilo !
She opened the door and let me in.
                                Hilo, boys, hilo !

Oh-o, I opened the door with a silver key,
                                Hilo, boys, hilo !
The yellow girl a-livo-lick-alimbo-lee.
                                Hilo, boys, hilo !

Oh-o, watchman, watchman, don't take me !
                                Hilo, boys, hilo !
For I have a wife and a large familee.
                                Hilo, boys, hilo !

Oh-o, two behind, and one before,
                                Hilo, boys, hilo !
And they marched me off to the watchhouse door.
                                Hilo, boys, hilo !

Oh-o, where's the man that bewitched the tureen ?
                                Hilo, boys, hilo !
Look in the galley and there you'll see him.
                                Hilo, boys, hilo !

Oh-o, the mate's on foc'sle, and the skipper's on the poop,
                                Hilo, boys, hilo !
And the cook's in the galley, playing with the soup.
                                Hilo, boys, hilo !

Oh-o, the geese like the gander and the ducks like the drake,
   Hilo, boys, hilo!
And sweet Judy Callaghan, I'd die for your sake.
   Hilo, boys, hilo!

"Oh, belay!" shouts the mate, cutting short the "shantie," for the yard is mastheaded. The main-topsail was next mastheaded, and the yard braced by, and then again came the order to man the windlass once again.

The chain comes in slowly for a few moments, and then stops altogether.

The crew strain at the windlass levers. The mate shouts encouragingly: "Hurrah, boys! Heave strong and break her out," and catching hold of a lever, he puts his own weight on it, calling to the men to "Heave away for homeward-bound. Heave another pawl, and she's all your own."

The windlass pawls drop slowly and with difficulty for about a minute, and at last:

"Hurrah, there she comes," and the anchor breaks out of the mud and clear of the ground, and now the chain cable comes rattling in quickly through the hawse-pipes.

The mate shouts aft to the skipper:

"Anchor's aweigh, sir," and in the same breath, "Haul back that slack chain, you boys; do you hear, there?" And the skipper sings out:

"Lay aft here, and swing the mainyard."

The after-yards are swung, and we are under weigh!

The ship's head pays off slowly, she points her bowsprit for the open sea, and we are homeward-bound at last!

But now we have to make sail, for as yet we have only set the fore and main-topsails, the two principal and heaviest sails in the ship; all is hurry and apparent confusion; orders are given and executed in quick succession.

"Hoist the jib."

"Haul out the spanker."

"Sheet home the main-topgallant sail."

"Man the halyards."

"Fore-topgallant sail there, the port watch."

"Hoist the flying-jib and fore-topmast stay-sail."

"Haul aft the main sheet," roars the skipper.

"Down foretack, our side," bawls the mate, and "Jump aloft, you boys, and loose the royals." And long before the sun shows himself we are clear of the harbour, and the old barque, under all sail, is bobbing her head up and down to the ocean swell; we are allowed half an hour to get our coffee, and then we muster all hands again on the forecastle to "cat and fish the anchor." We are fairly at sea now, heading westward with a pleasant breeze.

The second day out from Casilda we sight and

pass the Isle of Pines, and I think of Barney and his buried treasure, and the passage out, and wonder if there was any truth in his story. On the third day we sight Cape San Antonio, the western extremity of Cuba, and as we double it and head northwards towards the Gulf of Mexico, the last look that we get of the land where so many of our companions lie, is the lighthouse on the cape, glimmering away far down on our weather quarter.

CHAPTER XXIV.

Going north—Cold weather—Hardships of a sailor's life—
Reefing topsails—Calling the watch—In the Channel—
Painting ship—Towing up the Thames—In dock—Ashton
starts for home—My relations.

WE have to haul sharp on the wind now and beat up, for the north-east trade-winds are against us, but the Florida Gulf Stream is in our favour, and sets us rapidly northward.

Every day grew colder, and we were well to the northward before we got clear of the trades, and then we had cold, disagreeable weather, which we felt very much after coming out of the tropics, for Ashton and I had very little clothing, and it was mid-winter in the North Atlantic.

We now experienced some of the hardships of a sailor's life; many a time, day and night, were we roused out of our sleep with what got to be a quite familiar cry, "All hands reef topsails;" sometimes it was supplemented with, "Look sharp there before the masts go out of her."

Both Ashton and I had learned to steer, and we took our regular tricks at the helm, and steered with the crew in all weathers on the passage home; although the *Tyrer*, like all bluff-bowed vessels whose beam bears a large proportion to their length, was not an easy-steering ship in the best weather, and when running before a gale, she often required two men to steer her, and they had an anxious time, and had to be extremely watchful to keep her from broaching-to and sweeping her decks. I have since then seen vessels of four times her tonnage, but of finer lines, easily steered by one man in similar weather, and I have no doubt that these old short, heavily designed ships are obliged to heave-to in many a gale, even when it is a fair wind for them, and thus make long passages. Twice we were hove-to on the passage to England; once for three days under a close-reefed main-topsail and storm staysail, and with the helm lashed hard down, and the old ship lying over at an angle of thirty degrees.

One night we had a stiff north-wester, cold and wet. The men had been kept busy all the first watch shortening sail; all the small canvas had been taken in, the jib and mainsail stowed, and the first reef taken in the topsails; and when we went below at midnight, we were in hopes that the ship was snug for the rest of the night, and that our watch below would not be interrupted until eight bells, or four in the morning.

As we had no dry clothing, we wrung the water out of those we were wearing and put them on again, and lay down all standing, and covered ourselves over with blankets, and all the spare clothes that we could muster, to try and keep ourselves warm. We had been about an hour below, and were beginning to get some warmth into our limbs, and the steam was rising from our wet bed-clothes, when the ominous sound was heard:

Thump—thump—thump, three blows of a handspike on the deck above, followed by the long-drawn-out cry of the sailor, "A-l-l h-a-n-d-s," then sharply "Reef topsails. Do ye hear the news there?"

"Ay, ay," answer the men below, and we jump up and hurry on deck.

The old ship was lying over to the gale, dragging her lee chain-plates through the water, the wind whistling through the rigging, and a cold, sleety rain was falling, that felt as if it were cutting into our flesh as the wind drove it into our faces and against the backs of our hands, and the night was as dark as the proverbial pitch.

What with the noise and uproar of the sea and the wind, and the ship every now and again plunging her lee rail under water, and, as she struggled up again, dishing the sea and sending it rushing aft with irresistible force, sweeping everything with it that was not securely lashed, it was impossible to hear the orders of the skipper, and they had to be passed along from one to another.

"Are you all ready there, Meester O'Brien?"

"All ready, sir," answered the mate, while he called to the men to "Man the reef-tackles."

"Let go fore-topsail halyards."

"All gone, sir," shouts the second mate, casting them off the belaying-pin and letting them fly by the run, and down came the yard, and out went the weather reef-tackle, until some one sang out "Two blocks—belay all that."

"Now, lee reef-tackle there, men. Don't be afraid of a little water," shouts the mate, for the water is waist-high in the lee scuppers, and as we wade down into it to catch hold of the lee reef-tackle, the *Tyrer* makes another swooping plunge. The mate, who sees, or rather feels, it coming, shouts to the men: "Hold on, there, for your lives!" I just catch the half-smothered accents of his voice as the sea lifts me off the deck. "Done for at last. I am overboard," flashed through my mind. No—I strike against something and cling to it, and as the ship recovers herself, and lifts her lee rail once more out of the water, I find myself nearly my own height above it,

U

and clinging to the fore-topmast backstays. Several of the men were saved from going overboard by being caught in the fore rigging.

"Any one missing, there?" asks the mate.

"No, sir," he is answered.

"All right, then. Now is your chance, the sail is slack; quick with that reef-tackle."

In another moment it is hauled out and made fast.

"Steady the braces, there. Pass the word, two reefs."

And then we disappeared up the rigging, over the top, and scrambled on to the topsail yard, feeling in the darkness with our feet for the foot-rope before letting go our hold of the topmast rigging, for a false step would send us to eternity. The first man on the yard takes the place of honour, the weather earing, at the extremity of the yard; the second man goes to the lee earing; the others are distributed along the yard, picking up the sail and holding the reef-points. When the weather earing man begins to haul out his earing, he shouts to the others, "Light over to windward," and the men light, or pull, the reef-band of the sail up to windward to assist him. When he has passed a couple of turns of his earing, and can manage the rest alone, he shouts out, "Haul out to leeward," and the men along the yard repeat "Haul out to leeward," and pull the sail to leeward to get it taut along the yard. As soon as the lee earing is hauled out and passed, the reef-band stretched along the yard, the word is given by one of the men themselves, whoever first notes that the band is taut sings out, "Taut bands—tie away," and the men knot the reef-points round the yard. If there is more than one reef to be taken in, the last one must have the reef-band pulled well under the yard, the reef-point brought up abaft, and knotted to the fore part of the point, well on top of the yard.

For the information of my readers who have never been at sea in a sailing ship, I must say that the man at the earing sits astride, near the extremity of the yard, with one foot on the "Flemish horse" to steady himself, and holds on by his knees. He does not hold on to the top-sail lift with one hand and haul on the earing with the other, as some marine artists represent him in their drawings; he never would get through with his work in that way. In a strong breeze, or indeed in any breeze, he requires the use of both his hands at the weather earing, and often finds it difficult enough, even with the assistance of the man at the "dog's ear," as the man next inside him on the yard is called, to get his earing passed.

The earing is a piece of rope about half an inch in diameter, fastened to the cringles in the leech, or edge, of the sail, and by which the reefed portion of the sail is secured to the yardarm.

After taking two reefs in the fore-topsail, we went on deck. The reef-tackles were let go, braces slacked off, halyards stretched out and manned, and with a few good pulls the sail was set again, for it was now close-reefed, and there was very little canvas to hoist.

The same operation had to be gone through with the main-topsail, and as we reached the deck for the last time, the mate sang out "Grogs," and the hands mustered aft at the break of the poop, where the steward served out a glass of grog to each man, after which the mate gave the order:

"Go below the watch—watch on deck, coil up the ropes," and our watch was free to go below again, and wring the water out of our clothes, and rest until four o'clock.

We did not think it worth while to turn in again, so we sat down on the chests, and hauling out the beef kid and bread barge, we made a cold collation of salt beef and biscuit, followed by a smoke, and then one by one dropped off into an uneasy nap, when, thump—thump—thump, went the handspike on deck again, followed by the call of the watch:

"A-l-l-lar-bolines* ahoy—eight bells below there. Do you hear the news? Show leg — show leg there," answered morosely by some of the watch

* The larboard, or port watch.

below with: "We hear—we hear. Don't make such a —— noise," and we bundled on deck again, to take the watch from four to eight in the morning, and relieve the "Star-bolines," or starboard watch, who went below for that time.

After a voyage of fifty days, we sighted the rock of St. Agnes, one of the Scilly Islands, on a fine frosty morning, and as the breeze was very light, a Cornish fishing-boat came alongside early in the forenoon, and exchanged some fish and potatoes for ship's biscuit and salt beef. The tide was running up Channel, and that night we saw the Lizard light on our port-beam. For three days previous to making the land, the weather had been fine, and all hands had been employed scraping and painting the ship, so as to give her a tidy appearance going into port, and as the weather continued fine, and the wind fair, they were kept at it all the way up Channel.

Planks were slung over the sides, and we were set to work to scrape the barnacles and seaweed off, as far down as we could reach, with the scrapers fastened to boat-hook staffs, and then we scrubbed the sides with birch-brooms lengthened in the same manner.

On the fourth day from making the land-fall, we were off the North Foreland, where we picked up a pilot, and began beating up for the Thames.

All scraping, painting, and brasswork polishing had been finished, and the old hooker looked as if she had only just come out of dock.

At Gravesend the pilot left us, and another, that I heard the men call a "mud pilot," came on board; a steam-tug took us in tow, and all our sails were clewed up and furled; the jibboom was rigged in, the lower yards cock-billed, or tilted up on one side, the topsail yards braced fore and aft, brace-bumkins on the quarters unshipped, and everything prepared for going into dock; and then there was nothing more to do, going up the river, but look at the shore and shipping as we glided past them, and console ourselves with the thought that our hardships were at an end, for the present, and that we would soon be with our friends. That evening the ship was moored in the West India Dock and the crew went ashore, and I have never laid my eyes on any of them since.

The mate and the apprentices lived on board the ship in the dock, and Ashton and I were allowed to remain on board until we could communicate with our friends; they also lent Ashton sufficient to pay his railway fare from London to his home in the Midland county where his parents lived, and I accompanied him to the station and saw him off.

I had an uncle living at Woolwich, and a letter soon brought him aboard the ship to look for me. He was surprised at my appearance and surroundings, and promptly walked me off to a tailor's shop, and in half an hour I was transformed from a patched and ragged sailor into a more presentable being. I had no luggage, but went "flying light," as a sailor would say; we jumped into a cab and drove to London Bridge Station, and before I was an hour older I was sitting on a sofa with my kind aunt and cousins around me, holding my hands and looking into my face, listening to my story, or as much of it as I chose to tell them, and every now and again uttering an exclamation of surprise or incredulity as they looked from one to another, and then at me again, saying in their innocent simplicity : "Oh, how thankful you ought to be to have escaped such perils! Providence must have taken you under his special protection."

I have never heard anything more of my friend Ashton, although he promised to write to me; perhaps he became too ill to do so, for when I shook hands with him at the railway station I fear that he was far gone in consumption. I often suspected it in Cuba, and the hardships that he underwent there, and on the passage to England, must have aggravated it; still, he was always cheerful and in good spirits, and was never a day laid up while I knew him.

He was one of the few—the only one, to my knowledge—who never received a scratch during the campaign.

THE END.

F. M. EVANS AND CO., LIMITED, PRINTERS, CRYSTAL PALACE, S.E.

www.ingramcontent.com/pod-product-compliance
Lightning Source LLC
Chambersburg PA
CBHW022101230426
43672CB00008B/1239